SCENES
Keep
HAPPENING

More real-life snapshots of teen life

Mary Krell-Oishi

MERIWETHER PUBLISH
Colorado Springs, C

Meriwether Publishing Ltd., Publisher
PO Box 7710
Colorado Springs, CO 80933-7710

Editor: Theodore O. Zapel
Assistant editor: Audrey Scheck
Cover design: Jan Melvin

Library of Congress Cataloging-in-Publication Data

Krell-Oishi, Mary, 1953-
   Scenes keep happening : more real-life snapshots of teen lives / Mary Krell-Oishi
      p.   cm.
   ISBN 10: 1-56608-108-4   ISBN 13: 9781566081085
1. High school students--Drama. 2. Young adult drama, American. 3 Acting. I. Title
   PS3561.R425S34 2005
   812'.54--dc22

                              2005017339

      1   2   3   05   06   07

This book is dedicated to:
The Drama Teachers Association of Southern California
California Educational Theater Association
and
Theater Arts teachers everywhere.
We are professionals who have chosen to teach.

Table of Contents

Preface

In the many years I have been teaching high school theater, I have been privileged to know scores of theater educators from across the country and from other lands. While we all have different cultures, experiences and situations, we have one thing in common. Teens. From wherever they hail, the teen experience is one of commonality. Fitting in, acting out, boyfriends, girlfriends, tests, work, college. The list goes on in a variety of languages. I think you will find that the scripts within this book tap into these experiences and bring them to life on the stage.

For the theater educator who is looking for something new for their students that will challenge their skills without offending their parents, I believe you will enjoy the material in this new book. These scenes have been performed and tested on my own students and many theater students throughout Southern California. Let me take this moment to express my heartfelt thanks to my friends and colleagues in the Drama Teachers Association of Southern California and the California Educational Theater Association. These wonderful teachers have taken my scripts, tried them out on their own students and given me valuable feedback. Gai Jones, Janice Krell, Cindy Little, Kim O'Rourke, Joe Parrish, Ron Perry, Mark Scott and Amanda Swann are just a few in a long list who have been generous with their time and students in helping me craft this book.

A question has come up regarding my scripts for festivals. Some, such as the Fullerton College Festival, do not allow "scenes," but only "one-acts." For future reference, you can use these scripts in festivals. I do not consider them scenes, but instead they are complete one-acts with a beginning, middle and end. There is an arc to each story line, and when I write them I do not see them as a small part of a larger piece. They are, truly, one-acts. So, if questioned, please show them this preface.

As long as I teach I will continue to write for teens. They make me laugh, they make me tear up, they try my patience and they inspire me. As long as I work with young adults, the scenes will keep happening.

Mary Krell-Oishi
June 2005

Introduction

Mary Krell-Oishi is a true hero to hundreds of high school theater students across the country. Not only does she create scenarios and monologs to which young actors can relate readily, but she also writes in the language that teenagers hear all around them on a daily basis.

I have used Mary's scripts since the first collection appeared in print, and I am proud to say that we have a number of trophies on our shelves as a result of Mary's talents. The students in the Midwest relate to the scenes and monologs in Mary's books in the same way that my students do in Southern California.

An indication of a "classical playwright" is one whose works can be translated into any language and still "work." There is no question that "The Bully" and "Going to the Top," which are in this current volume, would be just as thought provoking and challenging in German, French, Spanish or Chinese as they are in English. People do not change from continent to continent, and the emotions, conflicts and wacky situations young people are embroiled in do not stop at national borders or state lines either. Mary has tapped into this universality with her keen eyes and open ears as she has traveled through teenage communities.

As a teacher herself, Mary Krell-Oishi knows how difficult it is to find suitable material for young actors for high school classrooms, stages, festivals and competitions. Often the language and situations in contemporary works are inappropriate and inaccessible for educational theater. These works are always appropriate, always accessible and always challenging for the actor; even more importantly is the fact that none of Mary's writing falls into the category of "cute!"

I am proud to be a colleague of Mary Krell-Oishi in my career as a theater educator. Having worked with her on numerous educational theater boards and committees, I know her to be a devoted teacher and an inspired playwright for youth in theater. I look forward to her work in the future as I continue to use her work from the past.

Kim O'Rourke
Representative for Trinity College, London-Guildhall Examinations
Vice-president California Educational Theater Association
Vice President California State Thespian Society
Board Member: Donna Reed Theater Foundation
Theater Chair: St. Lucy's Priory High School, Glendora, California

Five-Minute One-Acts

Alone Time

Cast: Marie, Alice
Setting: Inside Alice's house

1 MARIE: Alice? Alice? Are you here? Alice!!

2 ALICE: *(Entering)* **What?!**

3 MARIE: I called, but you didn't pick up.

4 ALICE: That's because I didn't want to talk.

5 MARIE: Why? I need to go to the mall and get some shoes to go

6   with that dress I got yesterday, the one with the stripes.

7   Remember?

8 ALICE: Yes. No.

9 MARIE: Yes what? No what?

10 ALICE: Yes, I remember. No, I don't want to go with you to get

11   shoes to match your new striped dress. We went to the

12   mall yesterday. Why didn't you just get the shoes then?

13 MARIE: I wasn't in a shoe mood.

14 ALICE: You're an idiot.

15 MARIE: So, get dressed and let's go.

16 ALICE: I don't feel like it. I'm tired of shopping.

17 MARIE: Have you lost your mind? Tired of shopping? Come on,

18   get dressed, put on some makeup and let's go. I'm driving.

19   I will even buy lunch.

20 ALICE: I don't feel like it. I just want to hang out at home.

21 MARIE: I'm offering to drive and feed you, and you don't want

22   to go? What are you going to do?

23 ALICE: I just want some alone time.

24 MARIE: Are you mad at me?

25 ALICE: No, Marie, I am not mad at you. Don't you ever just

26   want to be alone?

1   MARIE: I don't understand.
2   ALICE: You know, by yourself. Maybe read, take a long bath,
3   turn off the phone, ignore the internet.
4   MARIE: Turn off the phone? What? What if you miss a call?
5   ALICE: If it is important enough, they will call back.
6   MARIE: What if it's a guy?
7   ALICE: What if it is?
8   MARIE: OK, now you are talking crazy.
9   ALICE: Marie, sweetheart, listen to me. Sometimes it is nice
10   for me to just be quiet. To not have to talk, to be around
11   people, to interact. Sometimes I just enjoy being by
12   myself.
13 MARIE: You *are* mad at me.
14 ALICE: And sometimes things aren't about you.
15 MARIE: But if you don't want to be with me, to go shopping, to
16   eat a free lunch with me, that means you are mad at me.
17   Why?
18 ALICE: I'm not! I had an awful week, too much homework, too
19   many people talking to me ...
20 MARIE: Aha! ...
21 ALICE: *(Cutting MARIE off before she can finish)* Not just you,
22   just too much. I just want to take a long bath, read my
23   book and take a nap.
24 MARIE: Beyond my understanding. How long will all this take
25   you?
26 ALICE: I don't know.
27 MARIE: Will you be done with your alone time in, say, three
28   hours? I mean, honestly, how much time can you stand to
29   be by yourself?
30 ALICE: I don't know ... OK, three hours.
31 MARIE: Then I will pick you up at five o'clock. That gives you
32   another hour to dress.
33 ALICE: But ...
34 MARIE: No buts. If I am going to give you this time alone, then
35   you need to give me time together. And I want your shoe

1   opinion. *(ALICE starts to protest)* No! You are going. I'm not
2   going to have my best friend turn into some sort of loner
3   freak. Be ready at five o'clock. And you better be in a good
4   mood. None of that mid-day nap groggy attitude.
5 ALICE: Gosh, you're pushy.
6 MARIE: And wear something other than those tacky jeans.
7   We're going to the mall, not the park. *(As she leaves)* Love
8   you!
9 ALICE: Yeah, yeah. *(To herself)* Maybe I'll just have a pint of
10 Häagen-Dazs and watch TV.

Before the Party

Cast: Gina, Heather, Ilene
Setting: Outside of a party

1   GINA: Heather, I cannot believe I agreed to go with you
2   guys to this party.
3   HEATHER: Why is this such an enormous thing in your
4   life? It's one stupid party.
5   ILENE: Gina, you have got to go to at least one party in high
6   school that your parents don't know about.
7   HEATHER: Really. You don't see me or Ilene telling our
8   parents every little thing we do, now do you?
9   GINA: That is because you don't have my mother and
10   father. I have them. And I know what they would do if
11   they knew that I was here. They'd kill me.
12 ILENE: You see, this is the beauty of this plan. They will
13   never find out.
14 GINA: You don't know my parents.
15 HEATHER: Your mom and dad think you're spending the
16   night at my house. My mom and dad think that we are
17   spending the night at Ilene's.
18 ILENE: And my mom thinks that you and Heather are
19   coming with me to spend the weekend at my dad's
20   house. And considering that my mom and dad don't
21   communicate since the divorce ...
22 HEATHER: Not that they did before the divorce.
23 ILENE: True. We are as safe as in God's pocket.
24 HEATHER: Now, listen to me. Ilene and I have already been
25   to at least four parties this year. We already know a lot
26   of the senior guys.
27 GINA: Yeah, I know. Does that mean you're going to leave
28   me when we go in?
29 ILENE: No. We'll introduce you. These guys love us

1   freshman girls. And they are so much more mature
2   than the guys our own age.
3 GINA: This just doesn't feel right.
4 HEATHER: It will feel great once you get in there. Have a
5   couple of beers and loosen up.
6 GINA: I have to drink?
7 ILENE: No, you don't have to drink. Be the only person
8   there who doesn't. Never mind that you'll stand out
9   like a sore thumb.
10 HEATHER: Really. God forbid you should be even a little bit
11   cool.
12 GINA: Since when is it cool to drink?
13 ILENE: Oh, that's right. Go nine-oh-two-one-oh on us.
14   Preach a little.
15 GINA: I'm not preaching. I'm asking. Do I have to drink?
16 HEATHER: No, big baby, you don't *have* to. But it's more fun
17   if you do.
18 GINA: This is sounding really stupid.
19 ILENE: Is this? Dominic is going to be there.
20 GINA: And ... ?
21 HEATHER: He specifically asked us to bring you tonight.
22 GINA: He did?
23 ILENE: Yes he did. And he told me he thinks that you are
24   really cute.
25 GINA: No way.
26 HEATHER: Yes way. So, what's it gonna be? Are you going to
27   spend the entire night out here on the lawn in front of
28   the house where the most raging party you've ever seen
29   or heard is going on?
30 ILENE: Or are you going to make your move toward high
31   school popularity?
32 GINA: Popular, huh?
33 HEATHER: Once we're in with these senior guys, we have it
34   made for the rest of high school. We are in!
35 GINA: OK, I'll do it. And even if I get caught, it's the first

1   really bad thing I've ever done. The worst that will
2   happen is I'll get grounded. But I will have been with
3   Dominic. Worth it?
4 **HEATHER and ILENE:** Worth it!
5 **GINA:** *(Taking a deep breath)* Then let's go!

Being a Woman

Cast: Mary, Janice

Setting: Mary's bedroom

Costumes/Props: Mary is in jeans and a shirt. She changes into a skirt during the scene. Janice is in a skirt and shirt and puts on earrings. Both girls can have makeup compacts, or this can be mimed. The mirror they look into is the "fourth wall."

1   **MARY:** *(Calling off)* **Are you ready?**

2   **JANICE:** *(From off)* **Almost.**

3   **MARY: Hurry up.**

4   **JANICE: Don't tell me to hurry.**

5   **MARY: We're going to be late.**

6   **JANICE: You know hurrying me just makes me go slower.**

7   *(She enters putting on earrings)*

8   **MARY: You're wearing that?**

9   **JANICE: I have it on, don't I?**

10 **MARY: I thought we didn't have to get dressed up for this.**

11 **JANICE: This isn't dressed up. You want to see dressed up,**

12 **give me another half hour and I will totally dress up.**

13 **MARY: You are so much more dressed up than I am.**

14 **JANICE: I am always more dressed up than you.**

15 **MARY: I know. I hate that.**

16 **JANICE: If you put on a skirt with that top instead of the**

17 **jeans, then you would just have to change your shoes.**

18 **MARY: I don't want to wear a skirt.**

19 **JANICE: You'd feel more dressed.**

20 **MARY: Then I'd have to put on pantyhose.**

21 **JANICE: Naturally.**

22 **MARY: But it's too hot and humid for pantyhose.**

23 **JANICE: Well duh.**

24 **MARY: I hate this! Why do we have to worry about what we wear?**

1   JANICE: We're women. It goes with the territory.

2   MARY: Men don't have to. I guarantee you, most of the guys

3   will be wearing shorts and Hawaiian shirts, lucky guys.

4   JANICE: It's not easy being a woman. If it were, men would

5   do it.

6   MARY: Darn right.

7   JANICE: So, are you going to change the jeans for the skirt?

8   MARY: Yeah, I guess. Hang on while I change. *(She exits to*

9   *change.)*

10 JANICE: Excellent. That gives me time to re-do my eyes.

11 MARY: Your eyes look fine.

12 JANICE: Not for nighttime.

13 MARY: *(From off)* What?

14 JANICE: Eyes must be darker for nighttime. So must lips.

15 MARY: Who says?

16 JANICE: Society.

17 MARY: *(Re-entering)* How's this look?

18 JANICE: Better.

19 MARY: Just better?

20 JANICE: It looks fine.

21 MARY: Maybe I should wear a dress.

22 JANICE: The skirt is fine, goes nicely with the top. But you

23   need more makeup.

24 MARY: I'll only sweat it off.

25 JANICE: Glisten.

26 MARY: What?

27 JANICE: Men sweat. Women glisten.

28 MARY: Oh brother.

29 JANICE: Why do you fight it?

30 MARY: Why are there these double standards?

31 JANICE: It's not double standards. It is a simple matter of a

32   standard for a man and a standard for a woman. And

33   women set themselves higher standards.

34 MARY: And men are more comfortable. I want to wear

35   shorts and a Hawaiian shirt and no makeup.

1   JANICE: Go ahead.

2   MARY: And have everyone talking about me? Not a chance.

3   JANICE: There you go. The standards. They're not set by

4   men, they're set by women. The men won't care if you

5   wear shorts and a shirt and no makeup. Most of them

6   wouldn't notice.

7   MARY: I know. Women don't dress up for men. We dress up

8   to impress other women. It's all a contest. It's

9   ridiculous. We are our own worst enemies.

10 JANICE: Part of being a woman.

11 MARY: Bad luck.

12 JANICE: *(Finishing her lips with a flourish, looking at herself*

13   *in the mirror)* But the results are gorgeous!

14 MARY: *(Looking at JANICE's finished results, she sighs*

15   *heavily and looks at herself in the mirror.)* I give up. This

16   is as good as I get.

17 JANICE: You look fine.

18 MARY: Yeah. Great. Let's just go.

19 JANICE: Oh, perk up. We'll have fun. We can make fun of

20   the girls who aren't as dressed up as we are.

21 MARY: Yeah, and they can make fun of us for being

22   uncomfortable and sweaty.

23 JANICE: Glisteny. *(She smiles and exits. MARY takes one last*

24   *look and drags off after her mumbling.)*

The Cosmic Law

Cast: Gabby, Kelly
Setting: A school hallway
Props: A backpack full of books, a set of keys

1   **GABBY:** *(Rummaging wildly through her backpack and*
2   *books)* **I knew it! I just knew it! Where are they?**
3   **KELLY: What are you looking for?**
4   **GABBY: What am I always looking for?**
5   **KELLY: Ah. Your car keys. I can give you a ride.**
6   **GABBY: But then that would mean I would have to leave my**
7   **car in the school parking lot until I got off work. I don't**
8   **know, I think coming back here and finding my car**
9   **without tires, windows and radio would irritate my**
10   **parents.** *(She dumps the contents of her backpack on the*
11   *floor.)* **Where are they??**
12   **KELLY: You are always losing those things.**
13   **GABBY: Well, thank you, Kelly, for your helpful**
14   **observations.**
15   **KELLY: Sorry.**
16   **GABBY: Why? Because I am late, that's why. If I had plenty**
17   **of time to get to work, then they would magically**
18   **appear in my hand. The gods have decreed that my life**
19   **is miserable. It's some sort of cosmic law: Late? Keys**
20   **are lost.**
21   **KELLY: Cosmic law?**
22   **GABBY: Yes. You know, one of those things that seem to be**
23   **unquestionable rules of nature, unbeatable. Like ...**
24   **Prom night? Your hair frizzes.**
25   **KELLY: Oh, I see. Like camping somewhere without**
26   **plumbing facilities ... your monthly friend makes a**
27   **surprise appearance.**
28   **GABBY: Didn't study, pop quiz.**
29   **KELLY: Find the perfect guy, loves to shop, talk, cuddle.**

1   **GABBY and KELLY:**   Gay.

2   **KELLY:**   Cosmic law.

3   **GABBY:**   *(She shakes her bag.)* **Do you hear jingling?**

4   **KELLY:**   I never thought of life like that. That there are laws.

5   Like these overwhelmingly natural laws that govern

6   our life over which we have no control.

7   **GABBY:**   *(Shaking bag again)* **I am sure I hear jingling.**

8   **KELLY:**   Does that mean there really could be a God?

9   **GABBY:**   *(Shaking again)* **Shhhh. Listen ...**

10   **KELLY:**   It makes you think, doesn't it? I mean ... there must

11   be a power higher than we are. Like, we could be some

12   little amoeba in a petri dish in someone's science

13   project in a universe higher than ours. We could be just

14   one step away from being flushed down some great

15   atmospheric toilet, an experiment of a seventh grader

16   gone bad.

17   **GABBY:**   *(Standing)* **Oh, wait!!** *(She listens.)*

18   **KELLY:**   It's almost frightening in the enormity of all that

19   could be out there. Don't you think?

20   **GABBY:**   *(She begins to jump up and down.)* **Listen! Jingling.**

21   **I knew I heard jingling.** *(She pulls her keys from her*

22   *pocket triumphantly!)* **Aha!!! OK, I have *got* to go.**

23   **KELLY:**   So, what do you think?

24   **GABBY:**   About what?

25   **KELLY:**   The universality of our existence.

26   **GABBY:**   The what?

27   **KELLY:**   What you were talking about ... the cosmic laws, the

28   things that move us.

29   **GABBY:**   Honey, I just couldn't find my keys. OK, I'm outta

30   here. Meet me at Dylan's house at nine-thirty and we

31   are all going out dancing.

32   **KELLY:**   If the powers that be allow it, I will meet you there.

33   *(She goes off, appearing to think deep thoughts.)*

34   **GABBY:**   Your parents? What? Whatever. Just plan on being

35   there. Bye.

Decisions

Cast: Suzi, Michelle

Setting: A high school hallway

1   MICHELLE: Suzi, are you still going to class today?

2   SUZI: Of course I'm going to class. It's a school day. That's

3   what one usually does on a school day.

4   MICHELLE: I'm leaving.

5   SUZI: Where are you going?

6   MICHELLE: Home.

7   SUZI: What's wrong, don't you feel good?

8   MICHELLE: I'm fine. I just don't feel like going to class.

9   SUZI: Michelle, it's only September and you're cutting

10   school already? What are you going to tell your mom

11   when you get home?

12   MICHELLE: She's not home.

13   SUZI: Where is she?

14   MICHELLE: Working. She got a job.

15   SUZI: OK, so she's not home. What are you going to do

16   when the school calls?

17   MICHELLE: A machine calls, not a real person. I'll just say I

18   am home sick. That way it will be excused.

19   SUZI: Whatever. You better not get in the habit of this, you

20   know.

21   MICHELLE: I'm only a freshman. It's no big deal this early

22   in high school.

23   SUZI: Yeah, but once you get used to not going, it's really

24   easy to stop coming to school altogether.

25   MICHELLE: Like I care. No one is at home to keep track, the

26   school won't ever find out because I will clear it myself.

27   I'm home safe.

28   SUZI: You're going to end up just like your brother.

29   MICHELLE: What's wrong with Eric?

1   SUZI: Nothing that one extra year of high school won't fix.
2   Look at him. Nineteen and still at continuation school.
3   MICHELLE: That's him, not me. I'll be fine.
4   SUZI: My mom told me that when we got to high school,
5   things would be different.
6   MICHELLE: What do you mean?
7   SUZI: She said that friends I've had since kindergarten
8   would change, and we'd all go different ways. I guess
9   she was right.
10 MICHELLE: You act like I'm turning into a derelict or
11   something.
12 SUZI: No, Michelle, you're just making choices I don't want
13   to make. I want to get ahead, not be a waitress at Sizzler
14   when I'm forty.
15 MICHELLE: God, it's just one day of school.
16 SUZI: One day today. What about next time?
17 MICHELLE: Hey, it's my life. Leave me alone. You do your
18   thing, I'll do mine.
19 SUZI: You do your thing. I'm going to class.
20 MICHELLE: You're just a kiss up.
21 SUZI: *(As she exits)* Kiss this, Michelle. I'm going to class.

The Diet

Cast: Joni, Karen
Setting: Cafeteria
Props: A delicious looking dessert

1 JONI: Ohmigod, this is — mmmm. Ohhh! Karen, taste it.
2 KAREN: No, thanks.
3 JONI: Divine! Heaven! Angels are flying in from above with
4   this in their little harp playing hands. You've got to try
5   it!
6 KAREN: You know I can't.
7 JONI: Yeah you can.
8 KAREN: Joni, no, I can't.
9 JONI: One little piece of this heaven on a bun will not hurt
10   you.
11 KAREN: Does it have carbs in it?
12 JONI: Well, yeah ... ohmigod, are you *still* on that Atkins
13   diet?
14 KAREN: It is not a diet. It is a way of life.
15 JONI: So, you're never eating a dessert again?
16 KAREN: No.
17 JONI: Not even chocolate?
18 KAREN: Especially not chocolate.
19 JONI: So, all you're going to eat is meat?
20 KAREN: No, I eat veggies.
21 JONI: OK. So, no carbs. No dessert. No *chocolate?*
22 KAREN: Right.
23 JONI: Not even one teeny tiny little bite? *(She holds the fork*
24   *of the dessert in front of Karen.)* **Just one.**
25 KAREN: You are not being helpful.
26 JONI: Goodness, I envy your self-control. *(She downs the*
27   *bite.)*
28 KAREN: Two more sizes, that's eight more weeks, at least. I
29   am not going to Winter Formal with Joey looking like

1   Shamu's big sister!

2 JONI: He's not worth it. Not compared to this. Ohhh, what is

3   that — I can't quite identify, some kind of tang —

4   cinnamon? Allspice? You'll know in an instant, you're

5   the expert.

6 KAREN: I really can't.

7 JONI: It's like a little dart in the tongue — there, between the

8   chocolate and the butterscotch cream, some kind of —

9 KAREN: Chipotle.

10 JONI: You're kidding. That's a chili.

11 KAREN: Eight bucks a slice, it's probably chipotle. *(Beat)*

12 JONI: Chili in chocolate. Interesting.

13 KAREN: Just a hint of it. Adds brightness. *(A beat)* What do

14   you mean, he's not worth it?

15 JONI: Joke.

16 KAREN: No, it wasn't.

17 JONI: It's just, what's with this sudden obsession about

18   your weight? Now you can't even taste a dessert? It's a

19   high school dance, for crying out loud, not a

20   coronation.

21 KAREN: It's only eight more weeks. I can do anything for

22   eight weeks.

23 JONI: So, you are off this diet after Winter Formal?

24 KAREN: Again ... it is a way of life.

25 JONI: Your whole life? *(Beat)* What, are you crazy?

26 KAREN: Fine. Thanks for your generous and unconditional

27   support. It's appreciated. Now I have to ...

28 JONI: Settle down. Good grief, you're touchy these days.

29 KAREN: Must be the fat cells. Calling for help. "I'm

30   lonesome. I need some friends."

31 JONI: Or the chocolate withdrawals. *(She takes another bite.)*

32   I'm telling you, this isn't dessert, it is God's way of

33   saying, "Yes, heaven exists!" Ah, that is gooood!

34 KAREN: You left a bite.

35 JONI: It's too rich for one person. When something is this

1   good, it's wrong not to share it. Are you sure?

2 KAREN: Yes, I'm sure.

3 JONI: So, I guess this last little piece will just go to waste.

4 KAREN: Yes ... it will. I am stronger than the chocolate. *(A*

5   *moment passes, she then scoops up bite with her bare*

6   *hands and eats it whole.)* **OK, so chocolate is stronger**

7   **than me. Oh, what's one extra pound or two?**

A Friend

Cast: Lori, Martha

Setting: Inside Lori's house

Props: Purse, sweater

1   **LORI:** *(Calling out)* **Just a minute.** *(She answers door.)* **Oh, it's**
2   **you. What do you want?**
3   **MARTHA: My sweater and my purse you borrowed.**
4   **LORI: Just a minute, I'll get them.**
5   **MARTHA: They better be in the same condition they were**
6   **when I lent them to you.**
7   **LORI: You mean dirty and beat up? I had the decency to dry**
8   **clean the sweater and polish the purse.**
9   **MARTHA: Very amusing, Lori. You always have been quite**
10   **the comic.**
11   **LORI:** *(She returns with purse and sweater.)* **Here they are. I**
12   **don't know why I borrowed them in the first place.**
13   **They are really rather tacky, aren't they?**
14   **MARTHA: That's not what you said when you gave them to**
15   **me for Christmas last year.**
16   **LORI: And the joke is that you actually used them.**
17   **MARTHA: You had them last night.**
18   **LORI: I was feeling like being silly. It was part of my**
19   **costume.**
20   **MARTHA: Right. Listen, you have a great life. See ya.**
21   **LORI: Whatever.**
22   **MARTHA: You know, I hate when you say that. Whatever.**
23   **You always say it when you know you've been nasty.**
24   **LORI: Whatever.**
25   **MARTHA: See? I was right.**
26   **LORI: Listen, Martha, you're the one who has the problem.**
27   **You're the one who flipped out last night at the dance.**
28   **I don't know what happened, but you went nuts.**
29   **MARTHA: You don't know? Did it ever occur to you that I**

1   was interested in Jason?
2   LORI: Jason? No, I didn't even think about it.
3   MARTHA: And that right there sums up our problem,
4   doesn't it?
5   LORI: The fact that I danced with Jason?
6   MARTHA: No, the fact that you didn't even think about it.
7   You never think about anyone but yourself. I've been
8   your friend since sixth grade, and now I guess I've just
9   had enough.
10 LORI: You mean all this is because of a guy?
11 MARTHA: No, but it's just another example of how you
12   think only of yourself. I'm sick of it. I told you I liked
13   him and the first thing you did when we got to the
14   dance was hit on him. And this isn't the first time.
15 LORI: Martha, I'm sorry. I didn't realize how you felt.
16   Really. It won't happen again. I swear.
17 MARTHA: Yeah, well, you've said that before. I've had
18   enough.
19 LORI: So this is it? No argument? We're not friends
20   anymore?
21 MARTHA: Lori, I don't think you know the meaning of the
22   word. *(She leaves.)*
23 LORI: *(To herself)* Whatever.

Going Out

Cast: Cori, Diane

Setting: Inside Cori and Diane's house

Props: Phone

1 CORI: Diane, where are you going?

2 DIANE: What do you care?

3 CORI: Take a valium, sweetheart. I just asked.

4 DIANE: Then don't worry about it, OK? You don't have to

5   know everywhere I go and everything I do.

6 CORI: What wild hair crawled into your Cheerios today?

7 DIANE: Oh, clever, did you make that up yourself?

8 CORI: Diane, what is wrong with you?

9 DIANE: Why do you want to know where I am going?

10 CORI: To be perfectly honest, I don't care where you are

11   going. I was just trying to make conversation.

12 DIANE: And you expect me to believe that?

13 CORI: I don't expect anything. Go, have fun, do whatever,

14   but back off.

15 DIANE: Oh, you'd like that, wouldn't you? You'd like me to

16   leave you here all by yourself while I go off shopping,

17   isn't that true?

18 CORI: Is that where you're going? Shopping?

19 DIANE: Wouldn't you just love to know?

20 CORI: Not really, Diane. Forget I asked.

21 DIANE: No, Cori. I will not forget it. I know why you want to

22   know where I am going.

23 CORI: Then, please, fill me in. I am completely lost in this

24   conversation.

25 DIANE: We are not conversing. I am talking, you are

26   listening. Got it?

27 CORI: Fine. I'll listen.

28 DIANE: You're darn right you'll listen.

29 CORI: So, what's the problem?

1 DIANE: Don't act like you don't know. Don't pretend that
2   you don't want to know where I am going so you can
3   call Tony and tell him I'm gone so he can come over.
4   Don't assume I am so stupid as to fall into that trap.
5 CORI: Call Tony? Me? He's your boyfriend, not mine.
6 DIANE: I'm glad to see you realize that. And I intend to
7   keep it that way.
8 CORI: I'm hurt. You honestly think I would go behind your
9   back and try to get Tony? I thought we were better
10   friends than that.
11 DIANE: But Janice said ...
12 CORI: Janice? She's the one that's after Tony. Haven't you
13   seen her around him? It's sickening. She hangs all over
14   him.
15 DIANE: Janice? You think so?
16 CORI: Think about it. Remember at Julie's party?
17 DIANE: Now that you mention it, you're right. I'm going
18   over right now to give her a piece of my mind.
19 CORI: You better. No man is safe around that wench.
20 DIANE: I'm going right now. I'll talk to you later.
21 CORI: Don't let her get away with this! Do this for all the
22   girls with boyfriends. *(She hugs Diane, who leaves. Cori*
23   *goes to phone and dials.)* Hello? Tony? She's gone. Come
24   on over.

Homecoming Date

Cast: Susie, Elaine, Karen

Setting: Susie's house

1 SUSIE: Where's Karen?

2 ELAINE: I don't know. She said she'd meet us here.

3 SUSIE: If we are going to get our dresses for this stupid

4   dance, we need to do it today. I have to work this

5   weekend, and I have volleyball practice after school

6   everyday this week.

7 ELAINE: I have to work, too. And I have to study.

8 SUSIE: Study? For what? It's only October.

9 ELAINE: If I don't keep up with a regular schedule, I will

10   slack. The first semester of senior year is really

11   important, Susie.

12 SUSIE: Yeah. I suppose. Did you call Karen?

13 ELAINE: She said she'd meet us.

14 SUSIE: Why are we even doing this? I didn't want to go to

15   Homecoming. This was all Karen's idea.

16 ELAINE: Yeah, and now she doesn't even have a date.

17 SUSIE: What? She's going with Henry.

18 ELAINE: Correction. She *was* going with Henry. He can't

19   get off work.

20 SUSIE: Darn!

21 ELAINE: Totally.

22 SUSIE: The only reason I'm going to this stupid dance is

23   because Karen was all "Oh, we have to go to all the

24   dances this year."

25 ELAINE: I know!

26 SUSIE: Well, what's she going to do?

27 ELAINE: She better get a date!

28 SUSIE: Totally!!

29 KAREN: *(Entering, out of breath)* Sorry I'm late.

1   SUSIE: I was one minute from leaving.

2   KAREN: Well, soooory! I had to take care of some business.

3   ELAINE: So, are we going to the mall or what?

4   KAREN: Yes!

5   SUSIE: You've got a date? You're sure?

6   ELAINE: Susie!!

7   SUSIE: I'm just asking. 'Cause if Karen's not going, then I'm
8   telling Ben that I'm not going.

9   KAREN: I'm going, I'm going!

10 ELAINE: Thank God! Now let's go get something to eat, then
11   buy the dresses.

12 KAREN: I'm wearing pink. Like a princess.

13 SUSIE: So, who are you going with?

14 KAREN: Who?

15 SUSIE: Yes, who?

16 KAREN: Someone ...

17 ELAINE: Who?

18 SUSIE: Will he fit in with our group?

19 KAREN: Oh, yeah.

20 ELAINE: Who in our group doesn't have a date yet?

21 SUSIE: Yeah, who?

22 KAREN: Well, he's not really in our group.

23 ELAINE: Karen, who are you going to Homecoming with?

24 KAREN: Listen, if I tell you ...

25 SUSIE: What do you mean "if"? We either find out now or at
26   the dance next Saturday.

27 KAREN: I just want you to be supportive.

28 ELAINE: What? What's wrong with him? Is he deformed or
29   something? Does he have an eyeball in the middle of
30   his forehead?

31 KAREN: Shut up! Just be supportive.

32 SUSIE: Girl, you better tell us who you are going with.

33 KAREN: *(Taking a deep breath)* Jonathan.

34 SUSIE: Jonathan ... ?

35 ELAINE: Who's Jonathan?

1   KAREN: You know him. Blond hair. Blue eyes.

2   SUSIE: Jonathan ... wait a minute ... backstage Jonathan?

3   KAREN: Yes.

4   ELAINE: Who are you talking about ... ? Oh no! Not that

5   sophomore who works crew?

6   KAREN: I asked you to be supportive.

7   ELAINE: You're going to go to Homecoming with a

8   sophomore?

9   KAREN: He's sixteen! I'm seventeen.

10 ELAINE: You're a senior ... he's a sophomore!!!

11 KAREN: I asked you to be supportive.

12 SUSIE: I think he's cute.

13 ELAINE: He's a sophomore!

14 KAREN: He's an old sophomore!

15 ELAINE: So he was held back?

16 KAREN: No! His birthday is one of those weird ones, so he'd

17   either be a really young junior or a really old

18   sophomore.

19 SUSIE: He's tall, too.

20 KAREN: I know! He's taller than Henry! I can wear heels.

21 ELAINE: He's a sophomore!

22 KAREN: I know that, darn it. But Henry bailed, everyone

23   else is taken and I am going to go to this dance! I don't

24   care who I go with ...

25 ELAINE: Obviously ...

26 KAREN: And I would expect my friends to be supportive.

27 SUSIE: I think he's cute.

28 KAREN: Thank you.

29 SUSIE: Trade you Ben for Jonathan.

30 ELAINE: I can't believe you two.

31 SUSIE: A date's a date!

32 KAREN: We'll look really good in our pictures.

33 ELAINE: He's a sophomore.

34 SUSIE: Lighten up, Elaine.

35 ELAINE: Karen, haven't you got any pride at all?

1 SUSIE: She's got a date! That's all that matters.

2 KAREN: And no one stays with their dates at a dance

3   anyway. We all hang out together.

4 ELAINE: But a sophomore.

5 SUSIE: Karen, don't listen to her. Jonathan is cute, he'll

6   look great in a tux, you'll have a good time.

7 KAREN: Thank you, Susie. Now, Elaine, if you have

8   anything else negative to say, keep it to yourself. Try

9   being a friend, OK?

10 ELAINE: Fine.

11 SUSIE: So, are we going to the mall or not?

12 KAREN: Elaine?

13 ELAINE: Yeah, let's go.

14 KAREN: OK.

15 ELAINE: OK. *(After a pause)* I don't know what Charles is

16   going to say about Jonathan being in our group at this

17   dance.

18 KAREN: It was his idea.

19 ELAINE: Oh my goodness! A sophomore! Good Lord!

20 SUSIE: Just get in the car and shut up. *(To KAREN)*

21   Jonathan's hot! I don't care if he's a sophomore. I'm

22   serious about trading dates with you. You can have

23   Ben.

24 KAREN: No, I'm good. He is cute, isn't he?

It's All about the Pizza

Cast: Diana, Camille, Cori

Setting: The school hallway, right after lunch

1   DIANA: So, Josh said that he didn't want to see me anymore.

2   CAMILLE: Are you alright?

3   DIANA: Of course I'm alright. The only bummer is that he

4   broke up with me before I could break up with him.

5   CORI: See, Camille, I told you that Diana wanted to break

6   up with Josh.

7   DIANA: Exactly, Cori. The idiot beat me to the punch, that's

8   all.

9   CAMILLE: Well, I would be devastated if that happened to

10   me, especially in front of all those people.

11   CORI: No one heard.

12   CAMILLE: Yeah, but everyone saw. There you two were,

13   middle of the cafeteria.

14   CORI: I'm telling you, at that moment I wished I was a lip

15   reader.

16   DIANA: Nothing to hear. It's no big deal.

17   CAMILLE: So, what finally happened? I came in right when

18   you slapped him in the face with the pizza.

19   CORI: Classic.

20   DIANA: Did you like that? I thought it was a very nice touch.

21   Just the right touch of the dramatic, don't you think?

22   CAMILLE: From where I was standing, it was perfect.

23   DIANA: I swear, Josh is such a fool. Thinking that breaking

24   up with me in public would keep me from losing my

25   temper. What was going through his mind?

26   CORI: He soooo doesn't know you.

27   DIANA: Which is why we were doomed from the start.

28   CORI: I never understood what you two possibly had in

29   common.

1 DIANA: Eating.

2 CAMILLE: Ah, the food factor.

3 DIANA: We did have many fine meals together.

4 CORI: Universal bonding. You know, if the leaders of all

5   nations would all just sit down to a good dinner, this

6   old world would be a better place.

7 CAMILLE: May I remind you that Diana just publicly

8   slapped a man with a pizza slice?

9 CORI: Always exceptions to universal rules.

10 CAMILLE: Assault with Italian food.

11 DIANA: He deserved it.

12 CAMILLE: What, exactly, did he say?

13 CORI: Yes, how did he approach this situation?

14 DIANA: You want irony? He used exactly the same speech

15   that I had come up with the night before. Almost word

16   for word. Uncanny.

17 CAMILLE: Details, please.

18 DIANA: Well, he starts off with the ever popular, "Diana,

19   you know I think you are a wonderful person."

20 CORI: NO!

21 DIANA: Yes ... and in the middle of the cafeteria.

22   Surrounded by people.

23 CAMILLE: What did you say?

24 DIANA: Nothing. I *knew* what was coming, and I didn't

25   want to make it easy for him. So I let him talk on and

26   on, spouting cliches.

27 CAMILLE: "You'll always be special to me."

28 CORI: "I will always have a special place for you in my

29   heart."

30 CAMILLE: "These past few months have been so special to

31   me."

32 DIANA: And the always comforting, "You're too good for

33   me." Which, of course, is true.

34 CAMILLE: We've been telling you that forever.

35 CORI: What did you see in him in the first place?

1 DIANA: His mouth.

2 CORI: His mouth?

3 DIANA: Have you ever looked at his mouth?

4 CAMILLE: I'm not a mouth woman.

5 CORI: It's all about the shoulders for me.

6 CAMILLE: Forearms. That's what it is all about. With veins
7   that show the muscle. Forearms.

8 CORI: Broad shoulders in a white wife beater. Uh huh. Go,
9   girl!!

10 DIANA: Can we focus back here, please? Anyway, it was his
11   mouth. Just the right size. Not too big where when you
12   kissed he would swallow you, and yet not so small that
13   you wondered if he had to be hooked up to an IV to eat.
14   You know, very baby bear?

15 CAMILLE: Baby bear?

16 DIANA: Just right. *(The girls nod in understanding.)* So,
17   anyway, there we were, him breaking up with me ... just
18   moments before I was going to break up with him. I
19   was dumbfounded! So, I was standing there, watching
20   that adorable mouth saying all the things I was going to
21   say to him, and the next thing I knew, I felt myself
22   getting angrier and angrier and then, *bam!* My hand
23   moved out from my body, holding the pizza, and before
24   I knew it that pretty little mouth was covered in
25   pepperoni and cheese.

26 CORI: It was a great moment.

27 CAMILLE: Yeah, your favorite food used in your defense.
28   It's almost like the pizza took sides.

29 CORI: And you win!

30 DIANA: Yep. It's all about the pizza!

Poetic Justice

Cast: Tracy, Megan
Setting: Hallway at school

1　TRACY: Megan! What are you doing here?

2　MEGAN: Why?

3　TRACY: I thought you'd be at home.

4　MEGAN: Would it have made a difference to you if I hadn't
5　　　come?

6　TRACY: Yes, as a matter of fact. I wouldn't be here if I had
7　　　thought you were going to come.

8　MEGAN: Don't be stupid. You belong here as much as I do.

9　TRACY: More so.

10　MEGAN: *(There is a moment of tense silence between them.)*
11　　　So, are you excited?

12　TRACY: *(She sighs audibly in disgust.)*

13　MEGAN: Yeah, me, too.

14　TRACY: You can tell how I really don't care by the way I'm
15　　　ignoring, can't you? Or am I not being obvious about it?
16　　　Maybe this will clear it up for you. *(She turns her back*
17　　　*on Megan.)*

18　MEGAN: Good grief. *(She goes around to be face to face with*
19　　　*Tracy.)* We're both here. I'm not leaving ...

20　TRACY: And neither am I.

21　MEGAN: Then we need to deal with this.

22　TRACY: Really? How? How are we going to deal with this?

23　MEGAN: Maybe we should start with you getting over it.

24　TRACY: Over it? How do you expect me to "get over it"? You
25　　　take my journal of poetry, my private writings, my very
26　　　soul, and you hand them in to our English teacher as
27　　　your own. And then, when he says how wonderful they
28　　　are, how they are filled with angst and imagination and
29　　　beauty, you just sit there with a big smile on your face.

1 MEGAN: Yeah, but ...
2 TRACY: And then, when he says that he is entering one of
3   them in the Poetry Festival, you again say nothing!
4   Nothing! Not a freakin' word!
5 MEGAN: I didn't think it would win.
6 TRACY: What, you don't think I'm a good enough writer?
7 MEGAN: No, I don't think I am. No one has ever praised my
8   writing before, and when he did, it was kind of nice.
9 TRACY: But I *wrote* it!
10 MEGAN: Well, I kind of lost sight of that.
11 TRACY: Oh, good Lord!
12 MEGAN: But Mr. Nicholas entered one of yours, too.
13 TRACY: *They are both mine!!!*
14 MEGAN: Oh, yeah. Anyway ... and now, here we are, both of
15   us, interviewing for the finals of this Festival. Cool,
16   huh?
17 TRACY: Oh, way great.
18 MEGAN: And the prize money is a five thousand dollar
19   scholarship, which will come in really handy.
20 TRACY: You are not serious?!
21 MEGAN: Well, yeah! I mean, books are expensive.
22 TRACY: But you didn't write the poem.
23 MEGAN: They don't know that.
24 TRACY: And you are just going to waltz in there and say you
25   wrote it?
26 MEGAN: Well, yeah! I mean, really, how would it look if I
27   told them now that I *didn't* write it? I'd look like a liar.
28 TRACY: You *are* a liar.
29 MEGAN: Well, you're just mean.
30 TRACY: Mean? I'm mean? How am I *mean*?
31 MEGAN: OK, look at it this way. You're really smart, right?
32 TRACY: It goes without saying ...
33 MEGAN: And I'm not as smart as you ...
34 TRACY: Not even close ...
35 MEGAN: And you're sure to get a full scholarship to every

1   college you apply to, right?

2   TRACY: Maybe ...

3   MEGAN: No maybe's about it. You have a fifteen fifty SAT

4   and a four-point-oh, plus you are on ASB. So ...?

5   TRACY: OK, yeah, I'll probably get a full ride.

6   MEGAN: And I, with my three-point-oh and my eleven fifty

7   SAT will be lucky to get in to whatever college will

8   accept me.

9   TRACY: I'm with you.

10 MEGAN: And no chance of a scholarship.

11 TRACY: True.

12 MEGAN: Would you really deny me this opportunity? I

13   mean, really? Come on ...

14 TRACY: *(A long sigh, then resigned)* Fine.

15 MEGAN: Thanks, Tracy. Now, maybe you could explain this

16   poem to me before I go in for the interview? Because I

17   don't get it at all.

18 TRACY: Oh, good grief.

The Secret

Cast: Ann, Beth
Setting: The school hallway
Prop: A small box

1 ANN: *(Entering, sees BETH who immediately hides*
2   *something behind her back.)* **Beth, what's that?**
3 BETH: **What's what?**
4 ANN: **That thing you just slipped behind your back.**
5 BETH: **Oh ... nothing.**
6 ANN: **Then let me see it.**
7 BETH: **It's not important. Just leave things alone, OK?**
8 ANN: **What's the big deal? Are you doing something that**
9   **would get you in trouble?**
10 BETH: **Come on, Ann, you know me better than that.**
11 ANN: **I thought I did, but then again, I don't think I've ever**
12   **seen you be secretive with me.**
13 BETH: **Listen, it's no big deal. It's just this.** *(She shows her*
14   *the box.)*
15 ANN: *(Looking at it)* **What is it?**
16 BETH: **It's just a box, see ... nothing to worry about.**
17 ANN: **What's in it?**
18 BETH: **I showed you the box, what makes you think there is**
19   **anything in it?**
20 ANN: **Oh, I don't know. A box, hidden, now closed, being**
21   **held in a death grip by my friend who is obviously**
22   **nervous and upset at being caught with something she**
23   **shouldn't have. I guess I'm just being silly.** *(She grabs*
24   *for the box.)* **Let me see.**
25 BETH: **No!** *(ANN now has the box.)* **Ann, no, don't open ...**
26 ANN: *(On seeing what is in the box)* **What the ... ?**
27 BETH: **Don't say a word. Not a single word. I don't want to**
28   **hear it.**

1   ANN: Where did you get this? And why?

2   BETH: I got it from a friend.

3   ANN: Who? We have all the same friends. No one gave me

4   one of these.

5   BETH: Yeah, well, too bad. It's mine.

6   ANN: Are you going to use it?

7   BETH: I don't know. Maybe.

8   ANN: When? Where? With who?

9   BETH: Maybe tonight. And probably with Jeff.

10   ANN: Omigod! Omigod! Tonight? With Jeff?

11   BETH: I believe that's what I said.

12   ANN: Does your mom know?

13   BETH: *No!!* For heaven's sake, what am I? Stupid? And don't

14   you go opening your big mouth.

15   ANN: How does Jeff feel about this?

16   BETH: How do you think he feels?

17   ANN: Doesn't he worry about, you know, getting in trouble?

18   BETH: Don't worry. These things are foolproof.

19   ANN: For your sake, I hope so.

20   BETH: I gotta go now. I need to get ready for tonight. Ann,

21   do you need one?

22   ANN: Yeah, right. *(BETH starts to leave.)* Beth, yeah. Maybe I

23   do.

24   BETH: I'll ask Jane. She makes these fake I.D. cards really

25   well.

26   ANN: Great. Call me tomorrow and tell me if it worked.

27   BETH: I will. See you later!

Ten-Minute One-Acts

Alone on Prom Night

Cast: Joni, Keri, Anne
Setting: Inside Joni's house
Props: Three cell phones, Anne has a set of keys

1   *(JONI is on the phone talking in a warm friendly voice*
2   *while looking at KERI and ANNE with meaningful*
3   *glances that only three best friends can understand.)*
4   **JONI:** *(On the phone)* **Sure. Of course. Yeah, that was fun. I**
5   **always have fun with you. Me, too, thanks. Well ... yeah,**
6   **OK. Uh huh.** *(She laughs warmly while she rolls her eyes*
7   *towards KERI and ANNE.)* **OK ... I'll talk to you later.** *(She*
8   *hangs up the phone.)* **Loser. Well, Prom's next week and**
9   **I still don't have a date.**
10 **KERI: Brian didn't ask you?**
11 **JONI: No.**
12 **ANNE: Nice fake laugh.**
13 **JONI: Practice makes perfect.**
14 **KERI: So, what was he talking about?**
15 **JONI: Oh, about what a great time we had at Dylan's party**
16 **and lots of how much fun I am to "hang with," and blah**
17 **blah blah. But did he ask me to Prom? That would be**
18 **the big N-O.**
19 **ANNE: I hate the guys at this school.**
20 **KERI: What is their problem?**
21 **ANNE: I've had a date for every Prom! Senior year ...**
22 ***nothing!***
23 **JONI: I hate them!**
24 **KERI: Losers.**

1   JONI: I don't get it.

2   ANNE: I hear that Brian is waiting until seven days before

3   Prom to actually ask someone.

4   KERI: All that's going to be left are the ugly girls. *(She*

5   *pauses reflectively while KERI and ANNE look at her*

6   *aghast.)* That would include us, wouldn't it?

7   ANNE: We are so not ugly.

8   JONI: Totally?

9   KERI: Promise! Totally.

10   *(A pause)*

11   JONI: You're not lying to me are you?

12   KERI: I swear! You are way beautiful. We all are.

13   ANNE: This no date thing, however, is not good for the ego,

14   when you think about it.

15   KERI: The only thing I feel better about is that you two

16   don't have dates, either.

17   JONI: Great. Glad our bitterness makes you feel better.

18   KERI: You know what I mean.

19   ANNE: We should just ask guys from other schools since the

20   guys here are such complete jerks. I hate them!

21   KERI: What are you complaining about? You at least had a

22   date.

23   ANNE: Oh yeah, great. With Albert. Albert! Puh-leeeeeze.

24   JONI: He's a sophomore.

25   KERI: Well, at least he's male.

26   ANNE: Yeah, and fifteen.

27   JONI: He's a guy!

28   ANNE: You like him so much, you go with him.

29   KERI: Yeah, that will happen.

30   JONI: At least he's cute.

31   KERI: And fifteen.

32   JONI: And tall.

33   KERI: And fifteen. Hello! Fifteen.

34   JONI: I don't know, Anne. He might be your last chance.

35   ANNE: Pass the arsenic.

1 JONI: I can't believe we are going to be sitting at home on
2   Prom Night.
3 KERI: Prom Night!
4 ANNE: Alone.
5 KERI: Alone on Prom Night.
6 ANNE: I hate the guys at this school.
7 KERI: We should go anyway.
8 ANNE: Yeah. Sure.
9 KERI: I'm serious. The three of us should just go and have
10   a good time.
11 ANNE: I want to go, but I'm not desperate. *(JONI looks at*
12   *her.)* Well, not desperate enough to go with a
13   sophomore or with girls.
14 JONI: It's not desperate. It's a statement.
15 KERI: Of what? That we are such big losers and so repulsive
16   to men in general that the only people we can get to
17   take us to Prom is each other?
18 ANNE: I don't get it!! How can we not have been asked?
19   We're popular, and cool!
20 KERI: Everyone likes us!
21 ANNE: Everyone wants to be like us.
22 KERI: Everyone knows who we are.
23 ANNE: We are super cool girls.
24 KERI: What the heck, man?
25 ANNE: I know! I am so serious.
26 JONI: Maybe that's the problem.
27 ANNE: What?
28 JONI: That everyone knows who we are and assumes that
29   we have dates. That's why no one has asked us.
30 KERI: You think so?
31 JONI: Totally! I mean, think about it. Everyone knows who
32   we are, right?
33 KERI and ANNE: Right.
34 JONI: And we've all three been to every Prom since
35   freshman year, right?

1   KERI and ANNE: Right.

2   JONI: We've all had boyfriends, right?

3   KERI and ANNE: Yeah, sure. Lots of boyfriends.

4   JONI: So, we've been to all the Proms, we've all had

5   boyfriends, everyone knows us, we're cute, too, right?

6   KERI and ANNE: Like you even have to ask, of course, who's

7   cuter?

8   JONI: And we don't have dates, right?

9   KERI and ANNE: Right.

10   *(A pause)*

11   KERI: You're going somewhere with this, aren't you?

12   JONI: Yeah ... at least I thought so.

13   ANNE: So what's the bottom line here, then?

14   KERI: That Prom is next week and we don't have dates and

15   it looks like we might not.

16   JONI: Yep. So, what are we going to do?

17   ANNE: I'm not going with a sophomore.

18   KERI: At least you can say you were asked.

19   ANNE: By *Albert Gwaltney*. Big whoop.

20   JONI: Gah-ross

21   KERI: So beyond!

22   JONI: And the nerve of him!

23   KERI: He's not even cute.

24   ANNE: At least I was asked.

25   JONI: Good point.

26   KERI: Yeah.

27   JONI: Which brings us back to our original point. What are

28   we going to do about this?

29   *(A pause)*

30   KERI: How about this. We could ask guys from another

31   school. We could say that we've been actually *seeing*

32   these guys, and that's why we are not interested in

33   going to Prom with anyone from this school.

34   ANNE: And may I point out again ... they are losers.

35   KERI: Yes, they are.

1   JONI: But continue your train of thought.
2   KERI: OK. So, what we do is start mentioning these guys. A
3   lot.
4   ANNE: Get the word out, you mean.
5   JONI: Show we don't care that no one has asked us.
6   KERI: Exactly.
7   ANNE: So, we could tell people that these fictional guys ...
8   JONI: Not real guys?
9   ANNE: If we knew real guys we would have dates for Prom.
10 JONI: We could come up with real guys, couldn't we?
11 KERI: If we could come up with real guys, we'd have dates!
12 JONI: You two need to think about this. I mean, if we are
13   going to *say* we have dates, why don't we get some?
14 KERI: If we could get dates, then we wouldn't need these
15   fictional guys.
16 JONI: Between the three of us we must know *someone* who
17   we could go with.
18   *(A pause)*
19 ANNE: No one.
20 KERI: Joni, don't you have that really cute cousin?
21 JONI: Todd?
22 ANNE: Oh, yeah, he's a hottie! I'd like to tear me off a slice
23   of that!
24 KERI: And those friends of his. Mmmm mmmm. Yum.
25 JONI: Gay.
26 KERI: Of course.
27 ANNE: What the heck?
28 JONI: I am ready to resign myself to a life alone.
29 KERI: I say we make a decision right now.
30 ANNE: To do what? No one has asked us to Prom.
31 JONI: Albert ...
32 ANNE: No one worth going with.
33 KERI: Here are our choices. A. We stay home.
34 ANNE: Lame.
35 KERI: B. We go with just ourselves.

1   JONI: Who's going to make the signs we wear around our
2   necks that say "Loser"?
3   KERI: C. We ask the guys on our own.
4   ANNE: What?
5   JONI: Us ask the guys?
6   KERI: Why not?
7   JONI: Because it is *Prom!!!* The guy is supposed to ask.
8   KERI: Yeah? Well, I don't see them doing it, do you? I mean,
9   think about it. Of all the guys we know and hang out
10   with, who has actually asked a single person to Prom?
11 ANNE: Paul, Bill, Tony, Eddy ...
12 KERI: Yeah, but they've all asked sophomores and juniors.
13   They don't count. Fringe guys. The good guys in our
14   group are just standing around with their fingers up
15   their noses saying "duh."
16 JONI: Sad, but true.
17 KERI: So, why should we wait around? Do you want to go to
18   Prom?
19 ANNE: Yes!
20 JONI: Brian was supposed to ask me. He was telling
21   everyone he was going to ask me. You heard him.
22 ANNE: Yes I did. But that was two weeks ago and he still
23   hasn't. Keri has a point. Are we going to sit around and
24   wait for things to happen or are we going to go out and
25   *make* them happen?
26 KERI: Do you want to sit home alone on Prom Night?
27 JONI and ANNE: No!
28 KERI: Do you want a date? Do you?
29 JONI and ANNE: Yes!
30 KERI: I can't hear you!
31 JONI and ANNE: *(Louder)* Yes!!!
32 KERI: *(Like a cheerleader, full of enthusiasm and*
33   *encouragement)* Then, ladies, take out your cell phones
34   and let's start asking!
35 KERI, JONI and ANNE: *(Whipping out cell phones, full of*

1   *exuberant energy over having made a decision)* **Yeah!**
2   **Whooo! So cool!!**
3   *(A pause)*
4 **ANNE:** So, who should I call?
5 **JONI:** Yeah?
6 **KERI:** Huh. I hadn't thought that far. *(The cell phones close.)*
7   OK, here's what we will do. Joni, you will call Brian and
8   ask him to Prom.
9 **JONI:** What!?!?!?
10 **KERI:** You know he wants to ask you. He may think seven
11   days is enough time, but it isn't. He's an idiot because
12   he thinks all you have to do is put on the dress and go.
13   He's unaware of the prep time. So, call.
14 **JONI:** What do I say?
15 **ANNE:** Duh! You say, "Brian, do you want to go to Prom
16   with me?"
17 **JONI:** What if he says no?
18 **KERI:** He won't. He's just too darn lazy to do this himself, so
19   you have to take care of it for him. Anne, who are you
20   going to ask?
21 **ANNE:** Whoa. I don't know.
22 **KERI:** Ask Eric. He's cute, he's nice, he's sweet ...
23 **ANNE:** He's so quiet.
24 **KERI:** You're not going to Prom to talk, you're going to
25   Prom because it's your senior year. Call him.
26 **ANNE:** What about you? Who are you going to ask?
27 **KERI:** Mark.
28 **JONI:** Mark? Why?
29 **KERI:** Because I know he'll say yes. He's liked me since
30   seventh grade. He'll be thrilled. And I want to go to
31   Prom with my two best friends.
32 **ANNE:** For sure! And once we get there and are seen with
33   dates, then we can dump them and have fun!
34 **JONI:** Exactly.
35 **ANNE:** I am so annoyed that I have to do this.

1 **KERI: So am I, but I refuse to miss Prom because the guys**
2 **we hang out with are such lazy losers.**
3 **JONI: Seriously.**
4 **KERI: So, find your guy's number on your speed dials.**
5 *(They do.)* **Press call.** *(They do. Then, quietly because*
6 *phones have been answered)* **Now ask!**
7 **KERI, JONI, and ANNE, filling in the name of their guy: Hi**
8 **(Brian, Eric or Mark). Do you want to go to Prom with**
9 **me?**
10 **ANNE: Anne!**
11 **KERI: Keri!**
12 **JONI: Joni!**
13 *(They all look at each other annoyed because their voices*
14 *weren't immediately recognized.)*
15 **KERI, JONI, and ANNE:** *(Quietly to each other)* **Oh my god!**
16 *(Back on the phones, fake smiles and sweet voices)* **That**
17 **would be totally awesome.** *(They each trill a flirtatious*
18 *giggle.)* **OK, talk to you later, and we'll figure out details.**
19 *(They all hang up.)*
20 **ANNE: Well, that's done.**
21 **KERI: So annoying that we had to do that.**
22 **JONI: Well, we've got dates. Now the hard part. The dress.**
23 **To the mall?**
24 **Anne: I've got my keys in my hand already.**
25 **KERI: I've had a dress on hold at Nordstrom's for a week.**
26 **JONI: Let's go!**
27 **ANNE: I *hate* the guys at this school!**

The Bully

Cast: April, Julie

Setting: April and Julie are at a table in the library. The intimidation takes place at and around the table.

Props: Table, notebooks

1 **APRIL:** *(Mumbling)* **Darn!**
2   *(JULIE shifts uncomfortably, focusing on her own*
3   *business.)*
4 **APRIL:** *(Heavy sigh of annoyed disgust)* **Sheesh!** *(Turns to*
5   *look at JULIE.)*
6   *(JULIE looks up, sensing she is being looked at. Smiles*
7   *wanly at APRIL.)*
8 **APRIL:** What are you looking at?
9 **JULIE:** Nothing ...
10 **APRIL:** You calling me nothing?
11 **JULIE:** No ... I ...
12 **APRIL:** Why are you looking at me?
13 **JULIE:** I'm not. I was just ...
14 **APRIL:** Just what?
15 **JULIE:** Just ... I don't know ... looking.
16 **APRIL:** At me?
17 **JULIE:** No ... you made a sound.
18 **APRIL:** A sound? What kind of sound?
19 **JULIE:** A talking sound.
20 **APRIL:** A talking sound?
21 **JULIE:** Well ... talking. I heard talking.
22 **APRIL:** So? Was I talking to you?
23 **JULIE:** That's what I looked up to see.
24 **APRIL:** So you were looking at me!
25 **JULIE:** I guess.
26 **APRIL:** So when I asked you before what you were looking
27   at and you said nothing, you lied to me.

1 JULIE: No.

2 APRIL: So, you weren't looking at me?

3 JULIE: I wasn't looking at you ...

4 APRIL: Looking through me? What? Am I invisible?

5 JULIE: No! Wait! No ... I ... uh ...

6 APRIL: You want to take this outside?

7 JULIE: Outside? You mean like fight?

8 APRIL: Exactly.

9 JULIE: I just want to get my homework done and go home.

10 APRIL: What homework are you doing?

11 JULIE: Trig.

12 APRIL: Who do you have?

13 JULIE: Mr. Miller. Fourth period.

14 APRIL: I have him third.

15 JULIE: Oh. OK.

16 APRIL: So are you doing the same homework as I am?

17 JULIE: Yeah, I guess so. He likes to keep all of his classes

18   pretty much doing the same thing at the same time,

19   you know. *(She attempts a friendly smile.)*

20 APRIL: Does he?

21 JULIE: Yeah.

22 APRIL: And how do you know this?

23 JULIE: What?

24 APRIL: Are you and he good friends? Does he call you up

25   the night before each school day and confide in you

26   what the assignments are going to be?

27 JULIE: Uh ... no ...

28 APRIL: Are you his pet? His little student confidant?

29 JULIE: He puts the assignments on the board every day,

30   that's all. I mean, they're right there on the board.

31 APRIL: You saying I don't pay attention in class?

32 JULIE: I don't know. I don't even know you.

33 APRIL: You don't know me?

34 JULIE: Well, I know *of* you.

35 APRIL: *Of* me? What does that mean? *Of* me.

1 JULIE: Well, everyone knows who April Hailey is.
2 APRIL: You bet they do. And no one knows who you are,
3   right?
4 JULIE: Some people do.
5 APRIL: I don't know who you are. You're new.
6 JULIE: Yes. My name is Julie Chambers ...
7 APRIL: And I don't give a care who you are.
8 JULIE: OK.
9 APRIL: So shut up.
10 JULIE: OK.
11   *(APRIL and JULIE sit in silence for a moment.)*
12 APRIL: *(Eyeing JULIE, she mutters something under her*
13   *breath.)*
14 JULIE: What did you say?
15 APRIL: Nothing you want to hear.
16 JULIE: Oh ...
17 APRIL: Would you like to do something about it?
18 JULIE: *(Nervously)* No. I'm good.
19 APRIL: I bet you are. Always the good girl I bet, aren't you?
20 JULIE: I try.
21 APRIL: Thinking you're better than everyone else.
22 JULIE: Listen, April, I just want to do my homework and get
23   out.
24 APRIL: Let me see your homework.
25 JULIE: You mean copy it?
26 APRIL: I said see it.
27 JULIE: No. That would be cheating
28 APRIL: You calling me a cheat? You really want to go down
29   that road?
30 JULIE: What road?
31 APRIL: The road that leads to no return. Where I meet you
32   at the end of it and beat the hell out of you.
33 JULIE: You mean fight? That's the second time you've said
34   that.
35 APRIL: I will whup you.

1 JULIE: I don't think you will.
2 APRIL: Oh, I disagree.
3 JULIE: Disagree all you want, but I won't fight you.
4 APRIL: Hey, you said everyone knows me. Why do they, girl?
5   Why does everyone know me?
6 JULIE: Because you have a reputation of beating people up.
7 APRIL: It's not just a rep, it's a reality.
8 JULIE: You're not going to beat me up because I'm not
9   going to fight with you.
10 APRIL: What are you going to do? Go get Mr. Gibson? You
11   going to tell on me?
12 JULIE: Maybe.
13 APRIL: Look around. There's no one here but you and me.
14   *(JULIE looks around and then back at APRIL.)* **You gonna**
15   **cry?**
16 JULIE: *(Gathering her things together)* **No, I'm going to leave.**
17 APRIL: *(Blocking her way)* **I don't think so.**
18 JULIE: Get out of my way, April.
19 APRIL: Make me, Jooooleeee.
20 JULIE: How old are you?
21 APRIL: What?
22 JULIE: How old are you? Because you act like you're in third
23   grade.
24 APRIL: Girl, you are begging for it. Oh, I know. Your
25   mommy or daddy told you if you confront someone
26   who is a "bully" they will back down. Sorry, but they
27   lied.
28 JULIE: I'm not going to fight with you. You might think that
29   is a way to be socially involved, but I don't. You see, I'm
30   an adult. I am seventeen years old, not seven. I don't
31   know you, we've never talked before this moment, and
32   I was just sitting here. So, whatever psychological
33   problems you are having, deal with them in therapy
34   because I'm leaving.
35 APRIL: And I say you're not.

1   JULIE: You're going to have to physically stop me.
2   APRIL: *(Grabbing her)* **OK.**
3   JULIE: **Get your hands off of me.**
4   APRIL: **Make me.** *(Pushing her)* **Make me. Come on, make**
5   **me.**
6   JULIE: **I said don't touch me.**
7   APRIL: *(Goes to lightly slap Julie's face to intimidate her.)*
8   **Don't what? Don't do this? Or this? Or this?**
9   JULIE: *(Getting emotional)* **Stop it, April.**
10 APRIL: **Oh, gonna cry? Boo hoo? Are those tears?**
11 JULIE: *(She snaps, turns on APRIL, grabs her by the hair and*
12   *throws her on the ground. APRIL, taken by complete*
13   *surprise, falls on her back. JULIE jumps on top of her,*
14   *grabbing APRIL by the shoulders and pinning her down.*
15   *She speaks in an almost frightened voice, a warning.)* **I**
16   **told you to stop, didn't I? I warned you, but you**
17   **wouldn't listen.**
18 APRIL: *(Shocked)* **What the heck?**
19 JULIE: **You don't even know me. You have no idea who I am,**
20   **just some new girl that you can mess with.**
21 APRIL: *(She struggles to get JULIE off. JULIE is unmovable.)*
22   **Get off of me.**
23 JULIE: **Shut up. Shut it!** *(Grabbing April's face by the chin,*
24   *she brings her up close to her own face.)* **You messed**
25   **with the wrong girl.** *(She holds up her other hand.)* **See**
26   **this ring? You know how deep a scar this would leave**
27   **on your face?**
28 APRIL: **You wouldn't**
29 JULIE: **Don't be so sure. I could take you out. I could swipe**
30   **it right across your eye and blind you. I could cut your**
31   **nose right there** *(She touches APRIL's nose on the side.)*
32   **and leave a truly disfiguring scar.**
33 APRIL: *(Just as tough as JULIE)* **You wouldn't.**
34 JULIE: **Wouldn't I? Why do you think you don't know me? I**
35   **transferred here from Garr High School. They expelled**

1   me for fighting. You ever been to Garr? You ever been
2   around that area? You think you are so tough. You
3   people with your SAT classes and your honors classes,
4   you have it so easy here, April. Even your name is easy.
5   I could kill you just because your name is so annoying.
6   *(She gets up.)* But I won't.
7 APRIL: *(Starting to get up)* I'm not afraid of you.
8 JULIE: You should be. The last person I got into a fight with
9   is still home recovering. I told you I didn't want to fight,
10   but you didn't listen. You gonna listen now? Huh? Are
11   you?! *(She slaps APRIL as APRIL slapped her.)*
12 APRIL: Yeah ...
13 JULIE: I thought so. You spread the word. You leave me
14   alone, your friends leave me alone, stay away from me
15   and from the people I make friends with. I'm starting
16   over, and this is my last chance. You mess it up for me
17   and you will pay and pay big. I'll have nothing to lose if
18   I blow this chance and I will take you down with me.
19   Am I understood?
20 APRIL: Yeah ...
21 JULIE: Good. Now get your stuff and get out so I can finish
22   my homework.
23 APRIL: Fine. *(She gathers her things.)* I'll see you around.
24 JULIE: If that's a threat, I'd reconsider it. If it's an invitation
25   to be friends, don't make me laugh.
26 APRIL: Whatever. *(She starts to go.)*
27 JULIE: Oh, and April. It looks like bullies do back down
28   when confronted, doesn't it?

Different Paths

Cast: Ariana, Zana, Paria
Setting: Inside Paria's house
Prop: A cell phone

1 ARIANA: What time is it?

2 ZANA: It's about five minutes later than the last time you
3   asked what time it was.

4 PARIA: What is your problem, Ariana?

5 ARIANA: You know I have to be in by nine o'clock.

6 ZANA: Oh, grow up.

7 ARIANA: I am growing up.

8 PARIA: Not fast enough.

9 ARIANA: Faster than my mom and dad would like me to ...
10   at least that's what they are always telling me.

11 PARIA: Your mom and dad need to back off.

12 ZANA: For real.

13 ARIANA: My mom and dad are OK.

14 ZANA: Yeah ... whatever. Paria, did you bring your cell
15   phone?

16 PARIA: Of course.

17 ZANA: Let me borrow it for a sec. I need to call Joey.

18 PARIA: I thought he broke up with you.

19 ZANA: He did. That's why I am using your phone. He has my
20   number on caller ID. He doesn't know yours.

21 ARIANA: If you aren't going out with him anymore, why are
22   you calling him?

23 ZANA: To find out who he's with.

24 ARIANA: You guys aren't together. Why do you care?

25 ZANA: Why don't you shut up? How's that for a great idea?

26 PARIA: Jeez, Ariana, what's your problem?

27 ARIANA: Me? Zana is using your unidentifiable phone to
28   call Joey to find out who he's with, they aren't together

1   anymore, and I'm the one with the problem? OK.

2 ZANA: Listen, he may not want to be with me, but that

3   doesn't mean I don't want to be with him. And as long

4   as he is not with someone new, then there's a chance

5   we can get back together.

6 PARIA: Exactly.

7 ARIANA: But what if he is seeing someone new?

8 ZANA: Then I go kick her butt.

9 PARIA: Exactly. And we will be right there with you.

10 ZANA: 'Cause that's what friends do.

11 ARIANA: You're saying you want to fight some girl over

12   Joey?

13 ZANA: *(Belligerent)* Hey, are you judging me?

14 ARIANA: I just think it's stupid, that's all.

15 PARIA: Stupid? Why? She's fighting for what she believes in.

16 ARIANA: She's fighting over a guy. Puh-leeze.

17 ZANA: He's my guy. Broken up or not, he's still mine.

18 ARIANA: OK ...

19 PARIA: You got a problem with that?

20 ARIANA: I just think that fighting is stupid.

21 ZANA: You *are* judging me!

22 ARIANA: Since when do we fight other girls?

23 ZANA: Since I tell you to.

24 ARIANA: Since you tell me to? What is that about?

25 PARIA: Listen, mommy's girl, you need to decide who your

26   loyalties are with. Are you one of us or not?

27 ARIANA: We're friends. We've been friends forever.

28 PARIA: Doesn't seem like it too much anymore.

29 ARIANA: What are you talking about?

30 ZANA: When we go out, you say you can't go. When we just

31   want to hang out, you have to be somewhere else. When

32   we want to take off to the mall, you always have some

33   reason why you can't.

34 ARIANA: Yeah, well my reasons are my parents. They don't

35   like me to just hang out. And when you want to go to

1   the mall, you always are leaving during school instead

2   of waiting 'till after school.

3 PARIA: School is for losers.

4 ZANA: I hate this place. It's a huge waste of time.

5 PARIA: I was talking to my mom and told her I was going to

6   take the GED and leave at the semester.

7 ZANA: That's such a great idea.

8 ARIANA: Leave school? In your junior year?

9 PARIA: It doesn't matter one way or the other. Hell, girl, I've

10   cut so many classes this year that I wouldn't graduate

11   on time anyway unless I took night school. Which I am

12   definitely *not* doing!

13 ARIANA: And your mom is OK with this?

14 PARIA: Yes. She wants me to get a job anyway and start

15   paying rent.

16 ARIANA: You're only sixteen!!

17 PARIA: My mom was married when she was sixteen.

18 ZANA: Ariana, sixteen is old enough to grow up. Look at

19   Romeo and Juliet. They were only sixteen.

20 ARIANA: And look what happened to them. And to your

21   mom, Paria.

22 PARIA: What?

23 ARIANA: She got married at sixteen, had two kids, divorced

24   at twenty-one, married again at twenty-five, had

25   another kid, divorced again, and now she's living with

26   that guy.

27 PARIA: You better watch what you say about my mom.

28 ARIANA: You are not seriously considering dropping out of

29   school?

30 ZANA: It's not dropping out. It's taking a test then getting a

31   job. Growing up.

32 PARIA: Target is hiring full-time, too.

33 ZANA: That's a great job! Good discounts, too.

34 ARIANA: OK, wait a minute. First *(Indicating ZANA)* you're

35   talking about finding out who your ex-boyfriend is

1 seeing so you can go get in a fight with her, and then
2 you *(Indicating PARIA)* are talking about dropping out
3 of school and getting a job at Target. What about
4 school? What about college? And, Zana ... what about
5 dignity?
6 ZANA: Since when are you judge and jury over everyone's
7 lives?
8 ARIANA: You can't honestly think that it is a good idea to
9 get in a fight with another girl?
10 ZANA: If she's crossing my territory, yeah, I do. You got a
11 problem with that, we can take it out back right now.
12 ARIANA: And do what?
13 ZANA: Settle it.
14 ARIANA: Fight? With each other?
15 ZANA: I got no problem with that.
16 ARIANA: Paria, you're OK with this?
17 PARIA: Just take it outside. Don't do it in my house.
18 ARIANA: You can't be serious.
19 ZANA: Oh, yeah I can.
20 ARIANA: Why don't you just call the park and reserve your
21 trailer?
22 PARIA: You did *not* just say that.
23 ARIANA: What? You think I'm afraid of you? I'm not.
24 PARIA: I bet you are. Mommy's girl.
25 ARIANA: I may be a "mommy's girl," but at least I know
26 who my daddy is.
27 ZANA: *(Going for her)* How dare you!!
28 PARIA: *(Holding Zana back)* I said *not* in my house! *(To*
29 *ARIANA)* Ariana, I can't believe you just said that. That
30 was just wrong!
31 ARIANA: Yeah, well so are a lot of things that are being said
32 by both of you lately. Fighting, dropping out of school,
33 cutting classes, hanging out with guys that are such
34 losers. Those are not choices I am going to make.
35 ZANA: You're the loser. Little miss high and mighty,

1   thinking you're better than everyone else. You're so
2   locked in to doing exactly what your parents tell you to
3   that you can't think for yourself.
4 ARIANA: Of course I can. You expected me to go with you to
5   beat up some girl who might be seeing a he's-a-big-
6   giant-loser of a guy who doesn't want you anymore.
7 ZANA: Joey's not a loser.
8 ARIANA: He didn't even graduate from high school! And
9   what's he doing now?
10 PARIA: He works at Target. That's how I am getting my job.
11 ARIANA: And that makes it even worse. Is that all you two
12   want out of life? A future in a red shirt and loser guys?
13 PARIA: I won't be at Target forever. It's a job, though. I
14   won't be taking money from my mom, like you do. I'll
15   be paying my own way.
16 ARIANA: On five sixty-five an hour. That ought to keep you
17   in Mickey D's big meals.
18 ZANA: Your problem is you never had to take responsibility
19   for anything. Mommy and Daddy do it all for you. "Get
20   up, Ariana. Go to school, Ariana. Be home by nine
21   o'clock, Ariana. Who you going out with tonight,
22   Ariana? Leave a phone number where we can get you,
23   Ariana. Let us wipe your bottom for you, Ariana."
24 ARIANA: Screw you.
25 PARIA: Your problem is you're a big baby.
26 ARIANA: Your problem is that you are both too stupid to see
27   where you are headed.
28 PARIA: Get out of my house.
29 ARIANA: Fine.
30 ZANA: I knew that you'd end up being this way. Ever since
31   we were small, you always felt like you were better than
32   us.
33 ARIANA: No. I always knew it. I just hoped that you two
34   would want to achieve more than your parents have
35   and take a higher road. But, apparently you two have

1   chosen to head to a life of trash.

2 PARIA: It's different choices, Ariana, just different.

3 ZANA: We're ready to move on, you're not.

4 ARIANA: No, it's more than that. I want more out of life
5   than to work at a going nowhere job or to stalk some
6   guy who isn't worth the time it takes to dial his phone
7   number. I'm focused on the long-term future, you two
8   can't see two days ahead of what you want right now.

9 ZANA: You just think you are so much better, don't you?

10 ARIANA: *(A long look at both of them)* Yeah. I do.

11 ZANA: Watch your back, girl.

12 ARIANA: I'm really scared, Zana.

13 PARIA: She's serious. So am I.

14 ARIANA: So what? What's the worst that can happen? We
15   get in a fight? I get a black eye? Maybe get bruised up a
16   little? So? I'll still go to school, and then I will go to
17   college, and then I will meet someone worthy of me
18   who respects me. And it will all be on my terms. And at
19   the ten-year high school reunion, I'll feel great. But I
20   bet you two won't even be there 'cause you'll be too
21   embarrassed about what's become of your lives.

22 PARIA: You gotta be alone on the street sometime, girl.

23 ARIANA: I'm gonna be alone out there right now. You two
24   are big talk. But I'm the one who's got action. See ya in
25   the checkout line, Paria. And Zana ... I guess I'll look for
26   you on Ricki Lake. *(She leaves.)*

27 ZANA: Let's go kick her butt.

28 PARIA: *(After a moment)* No.

29 ZANA: No?

30 PARIA: *(Looking at ZANA for a moment, making a choice)* No.
31   I don't think I will. Not tonight.

32 ZANA: Well, at least come with me to cruise by Joey's house.

33 PARIA: Nope. Not that, either.

34 ZANA: What's up with you?

35 PARIA: I've got things to do. I have an early job interview

1   tomorrow.
2   **ZANA: But what if that girl is at Joey's house? What then?**
3   **PARIA: You do what you have to do.**
4   **ZANA: So, I'm on my own?**
5   **PARIA: I guess we all are.** *(She exits.)*
6   **ZANA:** *(Shakes her head in disbelief.)*

Fresh Air and Sunshine

Cast: Heather, Megan, Tamra, Becky, Jerusha
Setting: The girls are on a camping trip before leaving
on a tour of Europe.
Props: Tamra has a cell phone, Jerusha has several
lists on sheets of paper. They all have
backpacks.

1 HEATHER: *(Sarcastically)* Well, if this isn't just the most fun
2   I've ever had, then I guess it's been a little too long
3   since my last visit to the dentist.
4 MEGAN: Dirt. Everywhere there is dirt. I'm covered with
5   dirt. I hate dirt. Heather, don't I hate dirt?
6 HEATHER: Yes, Megan, you hate dirt. You've been sharing
7   your feelings about dirt for the last half hour. We all
8   now know that Megan hates dirt.
9 TAMRA: There are a lot of trees here, aren't there? Do you
10   think I'll be able to get a clear connection with my
11   cellular?
12 HEATHER: Who cares, Tamra?
13 MEGAN: I just want it clear that I hate dirt. Tamra, is there
14   a bug in my hair?
15 TAMRA: No, Megan, just the dirt. Todd's expecting me to
16   call.
17 MEGAN: I'm not happy here!
18 TAMRA: My cell phone isn't working. Maybe I need a new
19   battery.
20 HEATHER: Why did you bring that thing? It isn't going to
21   work all the way out here in the middle of this
22   godforsaken spot.
23 TAMRA: No one told me that I wouldn't be able to use a
24   phone! I wouldn't have come if I knew that.
25 MEGAN: What were you thinking, Tamra? It's called

1   "roughing it." Oh, wait, I forgot. Your idea of roughing
2   it is leaving your answer machine off.
3   HEATHER: Why are we here? What on earth made us
4   decide to do this?
5   MEGAN: What a stupid way to begin a summer in Europe.
6   Camping.
7   HEATHER: See America first? Oh puh-leeeze! Who's bright
8   idea was this, anyway?
9   BECKY: *(Enthusiastically and joyfully entering with*
10   *JERUSHA)* Isn't this great? I love camping. Mmmmm,
11   smell that fresh air.
12   JERUSHA: OK, everybody, gather around. I have the job
13   lists.
14   MEGAN: And who put you in charge, Jerusha?
15   JERUSHA: You know as well as I do that if I didn't organize
16   things, nothing would be done right.
17   TAMRA: You mean done the way you like it done.
18   JERUSHA: Same difference, Tamra.
19   HEATHER: The Jerusha way is the right way lately, it seems.
20   MEGAN: We're all getting a little tired of ...
21   BECKY: Come on, everyone, let's all be nice. We're going to
22   be together for the whole summer. Let's not start off by
23   arguing over silly things.
24   TAMRA: I am being nice, Becky. As nice as a person can be
25   when she leaves her only boyfriend to start a summer
26   tour of Europe by spending her last long weekend at
27   home lost in the woods with a bunch of girls. What was
28   I thinking?
29   JERUSHA: Tamra, it will be fun.
30   BECKY: Look around you. Isn't this a beautiful area? So
31   green and fresh. Let's try to appreciate where we are
32   and what we have. Look at the beauty that is America.
33   TAMRA: There are too many trees. They're blocking my cell
34   reception.
35   HEATHER: My feet are so swollen I can hardly get my shoes off.

1   MEGAN: There should be a place around here somewhere
2   with less dirt.
3   JERUSHA: It's called "camping out" ... out in the outside ...
4   where there's dirt on the ground. Otherwise it would
5   be called "camping in"!
6   HEATHER: In, out, who cares? Camping? Eeesh!
7   BECKY: This is a nice spot. But, if you want to, we can keep
8   hiking until we can find a place we all like.
9   HEATHER: Not on a bet. My feet are killing me. Look at this,
10   blisters!!
11   JERUSHA: If you had worn hiking boots like Becky and I
12   did you wouldn't be complaining now about sore feet.
13   HEATHER: Tell us Rush and Beck, what's it like to be
14   perfect?
15   TAMRA: Do you think if I stood over here where the trees
16   are more open I could get the phone to work?
17   MEGAN: Is there dirt on my back? I think I feel a twig
18   stabbing me in the back.
19   HEATHER: Well, something is stabbing us all in the back
20   and I think it's Mother Nature.
21   TAMRA: I think we should find a more open area ... you
22   know, so the sun would warm us.
23   JERUSHA: Are you still trying to make that phone work?
24   TAMRA: Hard to do when we're in the middle of nowhere.
25   HEATHER: Quit talking about the phone!!! Put it away, OK?
26   Just put the stupid thing away.
27   JERUSHA: Get used to it not working, Tamra.
28   TAMRA: What!?
29   JERUSHA: Well, you certainly don't think it's going to be
30   able to make a connection back to the U.S. from France
31   or Italy or England, do you?
32   TAMRA: What?!
33   BECKY: Your phone won't work there.
34   TAMRA: No phone? Are you insane?
35   HEATHER: So, what's the deal? Are we making camp here

1   or moving on? Personally, I'm getting tired of walking.

2   TAMRA: Megan, she's kidding about the phone not

3   working, right?

4   MEGAN: It's starting to get cold. Maybe we should just

5   camp here for the night.

6   TAMRA: I need to call Todd now and tell him. *(She looks*

7   *above at the offending trees.)* Rats!! Where's the stinking

8   sky?

9   BECKY: The ground looks pretty level here. We could pitch

10   tents under these trees.

11   TAMRA: Maybe my phone would work if we moved on.

12   JERUSHA: I know there's a better spot about a mile on

13   down a ways.

14   HEATHER: A mile?! I am not moving another inch let alone

15   another mile.

16   MEGAN: I'm with Heather. My feet are screaming for relief.

17   JERUSHA: If you had listened to me ...

18   HEATHER: If we had listened to me, we'd be back in our

19   own warm homes, resting comfortably before we leave

20   on a long trip.

21   BECKY: But what a boring way to spend the first days of a

22   vacation. We're young, energetic, we've got beautiful

23   country to explore.

24   MEGAN: Beautiful? Look around you. Not a hotel room in

25   sight, let alone room service ...

26   HEATHER: We have to pitch tents and sleep in sleeping

27   bags ...

28   TAMRA: Who knows what kind of bugs and animals will be

29   sniffing around us waiting to pounce and destroy ...

30   HEATHER: *(Examining her feet)* And look at this ... *blood.*

31   My feet are actually bleeding.

32   MEGAN: I think I'm getting cramps and we all know what

33   that means. And you show me where there's a

34   bathroom!

35   TAMRA: And my phone still doesn't work. This stinks.

1 **BECKY:** *(Starting to become more than a little irritated)* **Good**
2   **attitude. Here Jerusha and I plan a wonderful**
3   **beginning to what should be the experience of a**
4   **lifetime.**
5 **JERUSHA: We do all the buying, packing, planning,**
6   **arranging for rides ...**
7 **BECKY: Our moms are the ones who drive us up here and**
8   **make sure that everything is taken care of ...**
9 **JERUSHA: And what do we get from you ... our friends?**
10 **BECKY: We get grief.**
11 **JERUSHA: Thanks a lot.**
12 **HEATHER: OK, pity parade. Oh, poor Becky and Jerusha**
13   **surrounded by their ungrateful friends.**
14 **MEGAN: We didn't ask you to plan this, you know.**
15 **TAMRA: We should have stayed home.**
16 **MEGAN: Totally.**
17 **BECKY: Oh, that sounds like a lot of fun.**
18 **TAMRA: Or gone someplace that has some kind of**
19   **civilization surrounding it. Cell connections,**
20   **communication ...**
21 **MEGAN: But no, we end up surrounded by dirt ...**
22 **HEATHER: And bugs ...**
23 **TAMRA: And wild animals ...**
24 **HEATHER: And spiders ...**
25 **MEGAN: And no guys ...**
26 **TAMRA: And no phone!**
27 **JERUSHA:** *(Exploding)* **OK, everyone, sit! Sit down now!!!**
28 **BECKY: Yeah!** *(to JERUSHA)* **Why are they sitting?**
29 **JERUSHA: Because we need to bond.**
30 **TAMRA: Bond? I hate bonding.**
31 **MEGAN: Bonding is stupid.**
32 **HEATHER: What's the point? No one wants to stay here.**
33 **JERUSHA: We shouldn't need guys around, or phones. Real**
34   **friends just need to support each other.**
35 **BECKY: Jerusha's right. We are here as friends and we need**

1   to take the time *without boys* and *without phones* to
2   renew that friendship or else it will die.
3 JERUSHA: Friendships need to be nurtured.
4 HEATHER: We'll have six weeks together to bond. Why start
5   now? And why here?
6 MEGAN: We couldn't nurture indoors? Or maybe in a posh
7   resort with poolside service?
8 TAMRA: And indoor plumbing.
9 MEGAN: I can't stand being dirty. I'd kill for a shower.
10 JERUSHA: If you mention the dirt one more time, Megan, I
11   am going to kill you myself.
12 HEATHER: Really, just shut up about the stinking dirt.
13 JERUSHA: OK, that's enough! Here we are, all friends, and
14   what are we doing? Bickering about dirt and
15   bathrooms and phones.
16 BECKY: That's right! We have the beautiful open sky above
17   us, fresh clean air ...
18 MEGAN: *(Muttering)* And dirt.
19 JERUSHA: You could look at it as dirt, Megan, if that's what
20   you want to do. I look at is as God's blanket for the
21   Earth.
22 MEGAN: Oh, please, spare us.
23 JERUSHA: Sit down!!! Everyone!
24 BECKY: Now!!!
25 JERUSHA: Now, everyone hold hands.
26 HEATHER: God help us. Holding hands.
27 MEGAN: Why don't we all sing camp songs and tell stories.
28 BECKY: Just do as you're told. We are going to bond as good
29   friends or no one leaves here alive.
30 TAMRA: Getting a little tense, Becky, even for you.
31 BECKY: Sit! Now, everyone just be quiet. *(They all sit,*
32   *surprised.)* Hold hands and be quiet. *(They do so for a*
33   *few moments.)*
34 HEATHER: *(Quietly)* OK, now what?
35 BECKY: Just listen.

1 MEGAN: To what?

2 BECKY: To us.

3 TAMRA: But we're not saying anything.

4 JERUSHA: The point is exactly that. We shouldn't need
5   words to communicate.

6 TAMRA: Good thing, since the phone's not working ...

7 HEATHER: Oh, my goodness, how much more annoying
8   can you be?

9 BECKY: Don't make me hurt you, Tamra.

10 MEGAN: *(After another moment or two of silence)* **OK, I'm**
11   **done bonding. Can we find a shower now? Or at least a**
12   **semi-clean creek?**

13 JERUSHA: Just forget it. This is a waste of time ...

14 BECKY: Rush ...

15 JERUSHA: No. That's it. It's obvious that you and I are the
16   only ones who really want to be here, who really want
17   to be a part of nature. We're fighting a losing battle.

18 BECKY: Maybe we should just go. Let's just pack it up and
19   pack it in.

20 MEGAN: *(Jumping up)* **Good idea!**

21 HEATHER: Come on, you guys. Just calm down. No one
22   wants to leave.

23 MEGAN: *(Disagreeing)* **Mmmmm.**

24 BECKY: Yeah, right.

25 HEATHER: Megan, Rush and Becky have a point, you know.
26   They did go to a lot of trouble to put this together and
27   all any of us have done is complain.

28 MEGAN: I guess so.

29 JERUSHA: Look, we can take this weekend in the open
30   forest and look for the negatives or we can take the
31   beauty of what God has given us and be thankful for it.

32 BECKY: We're going to be spending six weeks together in
33   foreign countries. We should take some time and
34   appreciate what we have here in this country. And
35   appreciate what we have with each other.

1   MEGAN: As much as it pains me to say this, it is a kinda nice
2   way to start a vacation.
3   BECKY: See, you can get into this!
4   HEATHER: And it is pretty out here ... in a sort of rustic way.
5   MEGAN: And we will have all that time in hotels in Europe.
6   HEATHER: Meeting really cute guys with really cute
7   accents.
8   JERUSHA: Right. We start off with no frills, just the basics.
9   No plumbing, no men, just the open sky and each
10   other.
11 HEATHER: It could be fun.
12 MEGAN: And it is for just these two days and then we're on
13   the plane for parts unknown and men unmet ...
14 BECKY: So, do we stay or do we leave?
15 JERUSHA: Becky and I will do whatever you guys want to
16   do.
17 HEATHER: OK. I vote for staying.
18 MEGAN: Whatever, I'm fine either way, I guess.
19 HEATHER: Becky, Rush?
20 BECKY: I'm staying.
21 JERUSHA: I'll stay if everyone else wants to. I don't want
22   anyone to feel forced. Megan?
23 MEGAN: Yeah, OK. But I need to figure out something to
24   raise my sleeping bag off the ground. I'm sorry, but I
25   just can't sleep directly on dirt.
26 BECKY: I'll help you rig up a cot of some kind. *(She looks*
27   *over at TAMRA.)* Hey, Tam, what about you?
28 HEATHER: Tamra! Do you want to stay? *(They watch her as*
29   *she struggles to get her phone work.)*
30 MEGAN: She won't care. Just lay down her sleeping bag and
31   she'll eventually settle somewhere.
32 TAMRA: Hey!! If I stand over here on this rock and lean to
33   the left, with my leg in the air, my phone works!!
34 JERUSHA: So, I guess that's a sign. We stay.
35 JERUSHA, TAMRA, MEGAN, HEATHER and BECKY: We stay!

Job Preps

Cast: Margaret, Caroline, Bernadette, Melinda
Setting: Margaret, Caroline and Bernadette are at
Melinda's house helping Margaret find just the
right outfit to wear for her job interview.
Props: Margaret has a variety of different outfits,
Melinda has a purse with Oreos in it,
Bernadette has a bottle of water.

1   MARGARET: So, do you like this dress?
2   CAROLINE: It's fine.
3   BERNADETTE: Can we just make a decision and go?
4   MARGARET: I think it makes me look fat.
5   MELINDA: You look fine. Take the stupid thing and let's go.
6   MARGARET: My hips look like two overripe watermelons
7   wiggling away under this thing.
8   CAROLINE: Then don't use it, Margaret. Try on something
9   else.
10 BERNADETTE: I've got to get going ... Vinnie's waiting for
11   me ...
12 MELINDA: *(Cutting her off)* Vinnie's waiting for me ... Yeah,
13   we know, Bernadette. We don't care.
14 BERNADETTE: Jealous, Melinda?
15 CAROLINE: I'm starving.
16 MARGARET: I told you to eat before we came over to
17   Melinda's.
18 CAROLINE: I did eat. That was six hours ago. My
19   metabolism is normal, my food has been digested, my
20   blood sugar is dropping and so am I.
21 MELINDA: Stop complaining. *(Reaching in her purse)* Have
22   a cookie.
23 CAROLINE: I can't just eat a cookie. It's too dry. If I pass out,
24   I hold all of you responsible.
25 BERNADETTE: Oh, for heaven's sake. Eat the cookie.

1   CAROLINE: Dry? I'll choke to death.

2   MARGARET: Should I try on the red dress?

3   BERNADETTE: Here, drink some of my water to wash it
4   down with.

5   MELINDA: Take the one you have and let's get going. We all
6   have things to do.

7   CAROLINE: Melinda, give me something from the fridge.

8   MELINDA: My mom's dieting. There's nothing in there but
9   two pieces of sliced jicama and tofu.

10 CAROLINE: Never mind. Give me the cookie.

11 MARGARET: Give me a cookie, too.

12 CAROLINE: Oh, so now you're hungry, too?

13 MARGARET: Oreos? I don't really care for Oreos.

14 MELINDA: *(Reaching again into her purse)* How about a
15   Strawberry Newton?

16 CAROLINE: I want that.

17 BERNADETTE: You already took a bite out of the Oreo.

18 CAROLINE: I can't have both?

19 MELINDA: *(Flinging her purse to the floor in front of them)*
20   Oh, jeez, just help yourselves.

21 BERNADETTE: Hey! Don't put your mouth on my bottle.

22 MARGARET: I am going to try on the other one I left in the
23   bathroom. I'll be right back. *(Exits.)*

24 MELINDA: We are never going to get out of here.

25 BERNADETTE: Why are we even here? Does anyone care
26   less than I about what Margaret wears on her job
27   interview?

28 CAROLINE: *(Quietly)* Why is she bothering? She's not going
29   to get the job.

30 MARGARET: *(From Off-stage)* I can hear you, ya know.

31 CAROLINE: *(Loud enough to be heard)* You're not going to
32   get the job.

33 MARGARET: You don't know that.

34 BERNADETTE: Who cares? Can we go? Vinnie and I are
35   going to an accordion concert tonight.

1   MELINDA: Yeah, wouldn't want to be late for that.

2   BERNADETTE: *(Flatly, an old argument)* **Shut up.**

3   CAROLINE: Why are you even going in for this interview?

4   MARGARET: Why not?

5   MELINDA: How about lack of qualifications?

6   MARGARET: *(Coming out in the new dress)* **Please. How**

7   qualified do you have to be?

8   CAROLINE: Oh, let's see. You are applying for an aerobics

9   instructor job. Perhaps you should know aerobics.

10 MARGARET: You dance around, sweat and just shout out

11   the occasional "You go, girl!" or "Dig in! Dig in!" How

12   difficult can that be?

13 BERNADETTE: Well, when you drop dead of your stroke,

14   we can all use it as an excuse to buy a new black outfit.

15   You are the most out-of-shape person I know.

16 MARGARET: Am not.

17 BERNADETTE: Are too.

18 MARGARET: Not!

19 BERNADETTE: Are!

20 MARGARET: Not!

21 BERNADETTE: Are!

22 MARGARET: Not!

23 MELINDA: When you two are done with this witty

24   conversation, perhaps we can move on.

25 MARGARET: Listen. Maybe I should wear dance tights with

26   a little flowy skirt over it.

27 BERNADETTE: Bad fashion choice.

28 CAROLINE: I hope you get this job, just so I can see you

29   attempt to do aerobics.

30 MARGARET: You want to see? Come on, right now. Let's go.

31 CAROLINE: You'll drop dead right in front of us.

32 BERNADETTE: So, are you wearing the dress you have on?

33   It looks fine. Melinda, take me home.

34 MELINDA: You don't know she'd drop dead.

35 CAROLINE: Dead as a doornail. Dead as last season's shoes,

1   dead as dead person. Dead.

2   MARGARET: Shut up. I'll be fine.

3   BERNADETTE: Melinda, I have your keys, let's go.

4   MELINDA: Margaret, Caroline has a point. You know you

5   don't just stand there, you have to move with them.

6   MARGARET: I'm not stupid. I watch those exercise shows.

7   CAROLINE: From your couch.

8   BERNADETTE: If I'm late for that concert, Vinnie's mom

9   will never forgive me.

10   MARGARET: Have you ever done aerobics?

11   CAROLINE: A couple times. I don't live under a rock, ya

12   know.

13   BERNADETTE: She's playing lead accordion. I can't walk in

14   late. It would be rude.

15   MELINDA: Margaret, do you have a routine figured out?

16   MARGARET: For what?

17   MELINDA: What if they ask you to audition?

18   MARGARET: Audition??

19   CAROLINE: You're screwed.

20   BERNADETTE: Good. That's decided. Melinda, take me

21   home.

22   MARGARET: I can make something up, I guess.

23   CAROLINE: You're screwed.

24   MARGARET: I really want this job. Have you seen how

25   many cute guys go into this club?

26   MELINDA: We should help her out.

27   CAROLINE: How?

28   MARGARET: I remember some stuff from that Richard

29   Simmons video.

30   MELINDA: Do you have any oldies music?

31   CAROLINE: Why does she need music?

32   MELINDA: So she can lead us in an aerobics lesson and we

33   can help her out with some ideas.

34   BERNADETTE: That would involve sweat, wouldn't it?

35   MARGARET: How's this one? *(She names a song from the '50s.)*

1   BERNADETTE: Sweating? I sweat for no one.

2   MELINDA: You want a ride home?

3   BERNADETTE: Like twenty minutes ago.

4   MELINDA: Give us just a while to help Margaret out, then

5   we can go.

6   MARGARET: Come on, Bernadette. I need this job. My cash

7   is running low.

8   CAROLINE: That will happen when you spend it all on stuff

9   you don't need.

10 MARGARET: I needed that faux fur hat.

11 CAROLINE: Yeah. You really need to walk around with the

12   fake carcass of some poor animal perched on your

13   head.

14 MARGARET: Some of us care about fashion.

15 BERNADETTE: Some of us care about getting to our

16   appointments.

17 MELINDA: It's only an accordion concert. Unless Drew

18   Carey is hosting it, you will be missing nothing.

19 BERNADETTE: But Vinnie ...

20 MARGARET: Boyfriends come and go. Friends last a

21   lifetime.

22 BERNADETTE: A lovely Hallmark sentiment. You've got

23   one song, and then we have to go!

24 MARGARET: OK.

25 BERNADETTE: One song.

26 MELINDA: This will be fun. We can all use a good workout!

27 CAROLINE: I sense disaster.

28 MARGARET: You guys line up over here. *(CAROLINE,*

29   *MELINDA and BERNADETTE form a line facing*

30   *MARGARET.)* **Now, the song.** *(She pushes play and begins to*

31   *"do aerobics," CAROLINE, MELINDA and BERNADETTE*

32   *follow her frenetic moves.)* **Yeah! Go! Scoop down, scoop**

33   **down!** *(The music and routine should last a minimum of*

34   *two minutes, no longer than three before the last girl*

35   *drops out. As she continues, they all become out of*

1   *breath, dropping out, quitting. They sit in exhausted*
2   *silence for a moment, breathing heavily.)*
3   **CAROLINE:** *(Deadpanned)* **This was fun.**
4   **BERNADETTE:** **I have to take a shower. I'm sweating.**
5   **MELINDA:** **We're out of shape. Maybe we should all join a**
6   **gym.**
7   **CAROLINE:** **Just give me another cookie**
8   **MARGARET:** *(Gasping for breath)* **I wonder if that job at**
9   **Taco Bell is still open.**

Sisters

Cast: Michelle, Nicole, Sandy
Setting: Sandy, Michelle and Nicole's living room.
Props: Magazine, can of diet soda,
purse, letters, pile of clothes

1   *(MICHELLE sits on the couch, reading a magazine, as*

2   *NICOLE enters and sees the house is a bit of a mess.)*

3   **NICOLE: Well, you look relaxed. Busy day?**

4   **MICHELLE: Nicole, leave me alone!**

5   **NICOLE:** *(Sensing trouble)* **Is Sandy home yet?**

6   **MICHELLE: Nope.**

7   **NICOLE: Did she call?**

8   **MICHELLE: Nope.**

9   **NICOLE: OK.**

10 **MICHELLE: And she didn't leave a note, nor did she leave a**

11   **message on the machine. You know we're roommates,**

12   **not attached to one another at the hip.**

13 **NICOLE: Fine. She's not home. It's not that big a deal.**

14 **MICHELLE: Fine.** *(MICHELLE and NICOLE are silent for a*

15   *moment.)*

16 **NICOLE: So, did you get the job?**

17 **MICHELLE: I don't need this right now.**

18 **NICOLE: I'll take that as the big no.** *(MICHELLE ignores her,*

19   *drinking her diet soda.)* **Can you at least move your feet**

20   **so I can sit down?**

21 **MICHELLE: There's a chair not being used. Why do you**

22   **have to sit on the couch? I'm comfortable.**

23 **NICOLE: Michelle, let me explain. This is my couch. How is**

24   **it my couch? By the virtue of the fact that I have what is**

25   **known as a job. J-O-B.**

26 **MICHELLE: Yeah, yeah. You have a job. I'm the big loser**

27   **because I don't. You know I'm looking.**

28 **NICOLE: From the couch?**

1   MICHELLE: Get off my back, OK? I said I'm looking.
2   NICOLE: Well, Sandy will be home soon ...
3   MICHELLE: Great.
4   NICOLE: Lose the mood, OK? Take your dark cloud in your
5   own room.
6   MICHELLE: All I need is one more older sister bugging me.
7   SANDY: *(Entering, her arms filled with groceries)* **Someone**
8   **want to help me with these?**
9   NICOLE: *(MICHELLE doesn't move from the couch.)* **Yeah, let**
10   **me.**
11 SANDY: Hey, Michelle, did you get the job?
12 NICOLE: Ix-nay on the ob-jay.
13 SANDY: *(To MICHELLE)* **You didn't get it? How could you not**
14   **get it?**
15 NICOLE: She doesn't want to talk about it.
16 SANDY: She better talk about it. How could you not get that
17   job?
18 MICHELLE: I am so not in the mood for this.
19 SANDY: Well, my dear girl, you better get in the mood. *(To*
20   *NICOLE)* **Any mail?**
21 NICOLE: Did you even go on the interview?
22 MICHELLE: Yes, I went on the interview.
23 SANDY: Well, what happened?
24 MICHELLE: I'm not discussing it with you. Got that?
25 SANDY: Do you have your part of the rent for this month?
26 MICHELLE: I'll get it.
27 SANDY: *(Supplying the answer)* **No.**
28 NICOLE: You don't have the rent? How can you not have the
29   rent?
30 MICHELLE: Gee, I don't know, Nicole. Could it be because I
31   don't have a job?
32 SANDY: You were supposed to interview today.
33 MICHELLE: I did. Now leave me alone.
34 NICOLE: So, you went on the interview. OK, that's a step.
35   Did you make a good impression?

1   SANDY: Did you wear the rose colored dress?

2   NICOLE: Did you do something with your hair?

3   SANDY: I put those letters of recommendation in your

4   purse. Did you get them?

5   MICHELLE: Can you leave me alone now?

6   SANDY: You lost them, didn't you? You lost the letters. *(She*

7   *goes to MICHELLE's purse.)* How can you be so

8   irresponsible?

9   MICHELLE: Leave my purse alone. Give it to me. *(She grabs*

10   *it out of SANDY's hands.)* They are right here. *(She*

11   *throws them at SANDY.)*

12 SANDY: Did you go on that interview or not?

13 MICHELLE: Shut up.

14 NICOLE: Please tell me you haven't been sitting on this

15   couch all day long doing nothing.

16 SANDY: This is so typical. So typical. You are such a spoiled

17   little brat.

18 NICOLE: Why do you do these things? I thought you were

19   growing up.

20 SANDY: You know, you can't live here free forever. You have

21   to contribute, too.

22 MICHELLE: I know that.

23 NICOLE: Well, not going on that job interview is not a way

24   of showing that you know.

25 MICHELLE: I went on the stupid interview. I went.

26 SANDY: And what happened?

27 MICHELLE: Nothing happened. Nothing at all. I went, and

28   nothing happened.

29 NICOLE: Did you talk to Caroline?

30 MICHELLE: No.

31 NICOLE: I told you to talk to Caroline.

32 SANDY: She told you to talk to Caroline.

33 MICHELLE: I heard her, Sandy. You don't have to repeat

34   everything Nicole says. I'm not deaf.

35 SANDY: So, you went on the interview and didn't talk to

1   Caroline. This makes no sense.

2 MICHELLE: I went on the interview and didn't talk to
3   anyone.

4 NICOLE: No one?

5 MICHELLE: Nope.

6 NICOLE: Why? Why would you go all the way downtown
7   and not do the interview?

8 MICHELLE: Because of the sign in the front door when you
9   walk in.

10 SANDY: What sign? The company name? Does "Mass
11   Connections" offend you in some way?

12 MICHELLE: Not that sign. The sign that says, "We test for
13   drugs."

14 SANDY: So?

15 NICOLE: *(Realization)* Oh ...

16 SANDY: What? *(She looks at Michelle.)* Oh, man.

17 NICOLE: And how stupid are you, Michelle? I thought those
18   days were behind you.

19 SANDY: I told you, we both told you when you moved in
20   here, there would be no drugs.

21 MICHELLE: It's not drugs. It's a little pot.

22 SANDY: *(Her voice harder)* I said no drugs, Michelle. None.
23   Not even pot.

24 MICHELLE: I didn't smoke it here.

25 SANDY: I don't care where you smoke it, as long as you are
26   living under my roof, no drugs.

27 MICHELLE: Nicole, take a quick look at Sandy. I think she
28   just became our mother.

29 SANDY: I'm not kidding around.

30 MICHELLE: When did you become such a buzz kill?

31 NICOLE: Michelle, we made this clear. We don't do drugs.
32   We don't want a roommate that does.

33 MICHELLE: It's only pot, for God's sake. And I'm not a
34   "roommate," I'm your sister.

35 SANDY: Let me see your purse.

1   MICHELLE: What are you, the vice squad?

2   NICOLE: Sandy, leave it alone.

3   SANDY: Why? Why should I?

4   NICOLE: It's not worth the hassle.

5   SANDY: Quit forgiving every stupid thing she does, like you
6   always do. Hey, we pick up her slack, we pay her end of
7   the rent, she eats our food. I've said nothing this whole
8   time.

9   MICHELLE: Are you kidding? You haven't missed a chance
10   to give me the deep disappointed sigh, the slammed
11   refrigerator door when you see there's a diet soda
12   missing, the rolled eyes when a phone call is for me
13   and I haven't paid on the bill. Nicole's been supportive,
14   you've been judgmental.

15 SANDY: Judgmental! Judgmental? I think I have a right to
16   judge someone who thinks it's totally fine to live off her
17   older sisters and not contribute. I believe most people
18   would judge you to be a loser of the first rank.

19 NICOLE: This isn't getting us anywhere.

20 SANDY: Yeah, I think it is. I think this is a conversation long
21   overdue.

22 NICOLE: You don't have to yell. I'm not the one you're mad
23   at.

24 SANDY: I'm mad at both of you.

25 MICHELLE: Sandy spreads her anger to all the world. She's
26   generous that way.

27 SANDY: I want to see what's in your purse.

28 MICHELLE: Over my dead body.

29 SANDY: OK.

30 NICOLE: Stop it, both of you.

31 MICHELLE: Stay away from my stuff.

32 SANDY: Not a chance. *(She grabs for Michelle's purse, they*
33   *fight for it, but Sandy ends up with it.)*

34 MICHELLE: Stay out of my purse!!

35 SANDY: *(Taking out a small bag with a small amount of "pot")*

1   There you go.

2 NICOLE: Michelle, what are you thinking?

3 MICHELLE: So, it's a little pot. Not even an ounce.

4 SANDY: *(Mocking her)* A little pot. Not even an ounce.

5 MICHELLE: It's no big deal.

6 SANDY: Really? *(She leaves the room.)*

7 NICOLE: Why? Why would you do this?

8 MICHELLE: Honestly, what is the problem? You act like you
9   never did it.

10 NICOLE: OK, maybe when I was in high school. But those
11   days are over. You're twenty years old. Grow up.

12 MICHELLE: Yeah, I'm twenty. But that's not an adult. I'm
13   still a kid. I can't even buy a bottle of beer.

14 NICOLE: Really? Well, you're old enough to get picked up
15   for illegal drugs and be tried as an adult, so don't pull
16   the helpless kid excuse with me.

17 MICHELLE: It's a misdemeanor.

18 NICOLE: I don't believe you just said that.

19 SANDY: *(Re-entering, her arms filled with clothes)* Time to go.

20 MICHELLE: What are you doing with my clothes?

21 SANDY: You're moving out.

22 MICHELLE: What? Why?

23 SANDY: I told you, no drugs, no stupid behavior, get a job,
24   pay your part of the rent and other bills, and you could
25   live here. You have failed to live up to your end of the
26   bargain.

27 MICHELLE: Nicole ...

28 NICOLE: Sandy, don't you think you might be over-
29   reacting?

30 MICHELLE: Nicole, tell her she can't just throw me out.

31 SANDY: One of us is going, Nicole. Is it going to be the sister
32   who is the jobless drug user or the one who pays half
33   the bills?

34 NICOLE: Don't put me in the middle of this.

35 SANDY: There is no middle. There's right and wrong.

1 MICHELLE: It's a lousy little bag of pot.

2 SANDY: It's the principle.

3 MICHELLE: Nicole ... ?

4 NICOLE: Sandy is right. Yes, I'm judging you. We both told
5   you no drugs. You made a choice. Live with it ... but not
6   here.

7 MICHELLE: Where am I supposed to go?

8 SANDY: How about back to Mom's?

9 MICHELLE: You're serious?

10 SANDY: As a heart attack.

11 MICHELLE: Fine. If that's how you want it ...

12 SANDY: That's how you made it.

13 MICHELLE: I'll be out by the end of the week.

14 NICOLE: No. You'll be out today.

15 MICHELLE: What about my things?

16 NICOLE: Between my car, Sandy's and yours we can
17   manage.

18 MICHELLE: What am I going to tell Mom?

19 SANDY: That's not our problem.

20 MICHELLE: I knew I shouldn't have told you about the
21   drug test problem. I should have kept my mouth shut ...
22   or lied.

23 SANDY: You know what? Get help. Seek therapy. Do
24   something, because you are screwed up.

25 NICOLE: *(Trying to keep calm)* Why don't you just head on
26   over to Mom's or wherever you plan on living, and we
27   will get your things over to you. Just leave now.

28 MICHELLE: Fine. I'm out of here. I don't need you two and
29   your holier-than-thou attitudes. I'll let you know where
30   to send my things. *(She exits.)*

31 NICOLE: Do you think we did the right thing?

32 SANDY: Yes. *(She looks at NICOLE.)* Yes. And she'll know it
33   too, someday.

Three-and-a-Half Years!!! And I Am Sick of You

Cast: Annie, Jill, Katie, Stephanie, Sarah
Setting: A play rehearsal

1   *(ANNIE, JILL and KATIE are sitting on stage. STEPHANIE*
2   *enters.)*
3   **STEPHANIE:** *(Entering, looking confused)* **Do we have**
4   **rehearsal today?**
5   **KATIE: I guess so. Where is Sarah?**
6   **JILL: If she's not here in one minute, I'm leaving**
7   **ANNIE: I've got so many things to do that are so much more**
8   **important than being here at this stupid rehearsal.**
9   **Where is Sarah?**
10 **JILL: Who knows? She calls this stupid rehearsal and now**
11 **she's late. I hate her right now.**
12 **STEPHANIE: When did she call this rehearsal?**
13 **ANNIE: What?**
14 **STEPHANIE: I didn't even know we had rehearsal. I just**
15 **saw your cars here so I came in. Whatever.**
16 **ANNIE: Is Sarah coming or what?**
17 **JILL: I am *starving!***
18 **SARAH:** *(Entering)* **Sorry I'm late. Let's start.**
19 **ANNIE: That's it? Sorry? Whatever.**
20 **SARAH: My car wouldn't start, OK?! Sorry!**
21 **ANNIE: You and your car.**
22 **SARAH: What's your problem?**
23 **ANNIE: Nothing.**
24 **SARAH: OK, then ...**
25 **KATIE: Alright, let's get started so Jill and I can go get some**
26 **food!**
27 **JILL: Yeah! I'm starving!!!**
28 **SARAH: Let's go from "Did you really faint?" OK? Stephanie,**

1   hello?!? Are you with us?

2 ANNIE: I hate this scene.

3 JILL: I know! Why are we even doing this dumb scene?

4 ANNIE: It is so Drama One.

5 KATIE: Didn't we do this scene in Drama One when we

6   were freshman?

7 SARAH: Whether we did or not, who cares? Let's just start,

8   please. Stephanie, aren't you supposed to be Stage Left?

9 STEPHANIE: Stage Left, Stage Right, whatever. I wasn't

10   even sure we had rehearsal, so you're lucky I'm here at

11   all.

12 SARAH: How could you not know we had rehearsal? We

13   talked about it in class.

14 STEPHANIE: Hey! I was here before you, so lighten up.

15 SARAH: Are you memorized?

16 STEPHANIE: No.

17 SARAH: What?!

18 STEPHANIE: I could lie and say yes, but no, I'm not

19   memorized.

20 ANNIE: Great.

21 JILL: We are never going to get out of here. I'm going to

22   starve to death.

23 KATIE: Let's just run this thing so we can get out of here.

24 SARAH: Nice attitude, Katie. Very Advanced Drama.

25 ANNIE: Why are we wasting our time? Stephanie, you're not

26   memorized?

27 STEPHANIE: Didn't I just say that?

28 ANNIE: Katie? Jill? *(They both just shrug and mumble.)* **Why**

29   do I waste my time? I could be shopping!

30 JILL: Let's just run this once and go to the mall.

31 KATIE: Works for me.

32 STEPHANIE: I don't care.

33 SARAH: *No!* We are *not* running it once. We are running it

34   'til it's good.

35 KATIE: *(To JILL)* We're never going to eat.

1 STEPHANIE: I have to leave in twenty minutes.
2 SARAH: No! You're not.
3 STEPHANIE: Yeah, I am. I didn't even know I was supposed
4   to be here. I have to work.
5 SARAH: Screw work! You have the rest of your life to work.
6   This is the last scene you are ever doing for drama. Get
7   your priorities straight.
8 ANNIE: Doesn't it bother anyone but me and Sarah that this
9   is the last acting we're ever going to do? That we are
10   graduating and this is it? Don't you care?
11 KATIE: Whatever. I took this class for fun and this isn't fun.
12 JILL: Me, too.
13 STEPHANIE: I thought it was an easy A ...
14 SARAH: Stephanie, have you ever, in the last three years,
15   ever gotten an A in Drama?
16 STEPHANIE: No ...
17 SARAH: Then why would you still think it was an easy A?
18   Idiot!
19 ANNIE: Listen, I care about my last scene being something
20   I am proud of. So, let's work.
21 SARAH: I'm with Annie.
22 KATIE: Fine!!! Let's start then.
23 JILL: We've wasted all this time already.
24 SARAH: And we're on tomorrow. So let's do it. *(The girls*
25   *place themselves for the scene.)*
26 ANNIE: *(As Mary)* Rosalie, be sure you clean my shoes and
27   move my things to my room.
28 STEPHANIE: *(As Rosalie)* Mary Tilford! Who was your
29   French maid yesterday and who will wait upon you in
30   the hospital ...
31 ANNIE: What? *(She looks at SARAH, exasperated.)*
32 SARAH: Insane asylum ...
33 STEPHANIE: What?
34 SARAH: The line is "who will wait upon you in the insane
35   asylum ..."

1 KATIE: Insane asylum, hospital, same difference ...
2 JILL: Could you please let us get through this without
3   stopping us? I swear, all we ever do is get stopped. Just
4   run the thing.
5 ANNIE: But if the line isn't right then my line doesn't make
6   sense.
7 JILL: No one is going to notice anyway. This is such a stupid
8   scene the audience is just going to glaze over when
9   we're on.
10 ANNIE: Not if we're good.
11 KATIE: Which we won't be.
12 SARAH: Nice attitude, Katie.
13 KATIE: Stop me when I lie.
14 STEPHANIE: Fifteen minutes ...
15 SARAH: What?
16 STEPHANIE: I have to leave in fifteen minutes.
17 SARAH: Omigod!
18 ANNIE: Let's just power through this, please? I don't want
19   to get on stage in front of those Drama One students
20   and look stupid.
21 SARAH: If we had worked during class we wouldn't have to
22   be here now.
23 KATIE: It's too noisy in class.
24 JILL: Why do you always choose the noisiest place for us to
25   work?
26 SARAH: Why are you always late for class?
27 JILL: It's not my fault that class comes right after break. I
28   have to eat.
29 ANNIE: If you say anything else about eating, Jill, I am
30   going to ... oooohh!!!
31 JILL: Bring it on, shrimp.
32 ANNIE: You want it? It's brought!
33 KATIE: Stop being so stupid!
34 ANNIE: Who are you calling stupid?
35 KATIE: Both of you.

1   SARAH: You're all stupid!
2   STEPHANIE: This whole rehearsal is such a waste of time.
3   JILL: Darn right it is.
4   SARAH: I am so sick of all of you!
5   ANNIE: *(Tears of frustration)* It will be a relief to never work
6   with any of you again!
7   KATIE: Boo hoo, Annie. Turn on the tears, as usual.
8   ANNIE: Do you want me to beat you?
9   KATIE: Oh, please, I am begging you to hit me first. Begging
10   you!
11   *(They all start yelling at each other.)*
12   SARAH: Shut up!! Just shut up! You know what? We've all
13   been in class together since our freshman year. This is
14   our last scene together. And you know what? I am sick
15   of all of you! I can't wait 'til graduation. I've had it with
16   you all.
17   KATIE: No kidding! I just want out!
18   ANNIE: Out! What a beautiful word.
19   STEPHANIE: No more school.
20   JILL: Freedom!
21   SARAH: I'll never have to work with any of you again.
22   STEPHANIE: Ever!
23   JILL: What a relief that will be!
24   ANNIE: I can't wait.
25   KATIE: Neither can I!
26   SARAH: One more week and we're outta here.
27   ANNIE: One more week.
28   JILL: And we're gone.
29   KATIE: Gone.
30   STEPHANIE: Out of high school.
31   *(They all stop and look at each other.)*
32   SARAH: One more week. That's all that's left.
33   ANNIE: We're never going to work together again.
34   JILL: Four years, gone.
35   KATIE: I can't believe it.

1   STEPHANIE: Four years.

2   ANNIE: Omigod! I'm going to miss you all.

3   SARAH: So am I!

4   *(They all fall into each other's arms, teary and*

5   *sentimental.)*

6   ANNIE: I can't believe that we are going to graduate.

7   KATIE: This is so weird. This time next year who knows

8   where we will be? I mean, Caitlyn graduated last year

9   and she got married last weekend.

10 SARAH: I know! What's up with that?

11 STEPHANIE: Things change so fast.

12 ANNIE: I am going to so miss you all.

13 KATIE: So am I! I'm going to miss this class, everything.

14 JILL: Me, too. I love you guys.

15 ANNIE: So do I! We'll never have these opportunities again.

16 SARAH: We should treasure this last time together.

17 ANNIE: We should! We should do this scene the best it's

18   ever been done.

19 SARAH: Let's give it one hundred percent. We'll work on it

20   until it is perfect!

21 ANNIE: Perfect!

22 KATIE: Wellll ...

23 SARAH: What?

24 KATIE: Do you really think that staying longer will make it

25   better?

26 JILL: I'm not really that great on an empty stomach.

27 STEPHANIE: I have to leave, remember?

28 ANNIE: Oh, good grief!

29 JILL: I told you I was starving.

30 ANNIE: This is such a waste of my time.

31 SARAH: So, let's run this at least once, OK?

32 STEPHANIE: I have to leave.

33 ANNIE: You have got to be kidding me!

34 STEPHANIE: Well, if we hadn't wasted all this time we

35   could have run it.

1   **JILL:** I'm starving.

2   **KATIE:** Let's just go.

3   **SARAH:** We're gonna fail this scene!

4   **JILL:** We'll be fine.

5   **SARAH:** I swear to God, three-and-a-half years and I am

6   sick of you!

7   *(They all start yelling at each other.)*

8   **ALL:** Shut up! You shut up! *Argh!!!*

9   *(They all exit in different directions.)*

Whiney, Lazy, Demanding

Cast: Jenilee, Brittney, Caitlin
Setting: Brittney's messy bedroom
Prop: Caitlin has a list

1 JENILEE: What are we doing today?

2 BRITTNEY: Nothing.

3 JENILEE: Again?

4 BRITTNEY: You can do something. I'm doing nothing.

5 JENILEE: I'm tired of doing nothing.

6 BRITTNEY: Wait a few minutes. Caitlin will be here and

7   she'll plan your day for you.

8 JENILEE: She always makes me do stuff I don't want to do.

9 BRITTNEY: No one is forcing you.

10 JENILEE: Caitlin will. I can't fight her.

11 BRITTNEY: I don't even try. Why bother?

12 CAITLIN: *(Entering)* Try what?

13 BRITTNEY: To argue with you.

14 CAITLIN: You won't win, so don't bother. So, you guys

15   ready?

16 JENILEE: For what?

17 CAITLIN: It's one of our few days off from school, from

18   rehearsal, from work.

19 BRITTNEY: Thank God!

20 CAITLIN: So, I've made plans!! *(She triumphantly whips out*

21   *a list.)*

22 BRITTNEY: Oh good Lord.

23 JENILEE: I told you.

24 CAITLIN: First, we help Brittney clean this disgusting mess

25   she calls a room.

26 BRITTNEY: It's not a mess, its comfortable.

27 CAITLIN: It's a mess. I don't know how you live in this filth.

28 BRITTNEY: I like it.

1   JENILEE: Speaking of which, I left my sweater here last
2   week. Have you seen it?
3   BRITTNEY: Look under that pile of clothes.
4   CAITLIN: You can look for it later. I'll add it to the list.
5   JENILEE: Why can't I look for it now? We're here now.
6   CAITLIN: Because if we don't follow the list, nothing will
7   get done according to schedule.
8   BRITTNEY: Whose schedule?
9   CAITLIN: Mine, of course. Unless either one of you went to
10   the trouble to make a list. Jen? Brit?
11 JENILEE: No, no list.
12 BRITTNEY: I'm going to take a nap.
13 CAITLIN: No, you're not. I swear, you'd sleep the day away if
14   I let you.
15 BRITTNEY: Let me?
16 CAITLIN: You're like a cat. All you do is eat, sleep and poop.
17 BRITTNEY: I bet you think that's an insult, but it's not.
18 JENILEE: What's on the list?
19 CAITLIN: Well, because we are your friends, Brittney,
20   Jenilee and I are going to help you clean this room.
21 JENILEE: *(Not at all pleased)* **Great.**
22 BRITTNEY: I don't want you to.
23 CAITLIN: Well, too bad. Your mom called me and asked me
24   to get you going.
25 BRITTNEY: What? Are you serious?
26 CAITLIN: Look around you. I can barely see the color of the
27   carpet for all the stuff on the floor.
28 BRITTNEY: *(Falling back onto the bed)* **Blech.** I don't want
29   to.
30 CAITLIN: Well, we're going to.
31 JENILEE: Why do I have to? It's not my stuff.
32 CAITLIN: Because I want us to, I care that my friend lives in
33   this squalor and it bugs me.
34 BRITTNEY: It doesn't bug me.
35 CAITLIN: But it bugs me, and that's what matters, right?

1   BRITTNEY: I give up. We'll clean.

2   CAITLIN: Smart girl.

3   JENILEE: What else is on the list.

4   CAITLIN: OK, first we clean, then we are going to lunch,
5   then the movies.

6   JENILEE: I want Korean Barbecue.

7   BRITTNEY: That new Adam Sandler movie is playing. I've
8   been wanting to see it.

9   CAITLIN: We're going to the Greek place and we are going
10   to the Mesa and seeing the *Gone with the Wind* revival.

11 JENILEE: What? Why?

12 BRITTNEY: That's stupid.

13 JENILEE: I want Korean.

14 BRITTNEY: Caitlin, you've always had it against Adam
15   Sandler.

16 JENILEE: Why Greek? Why not Korean? Racist.

17 BRITTNEY: And the Mesa is all the way down in
18   Huntington Beach.

19 JENILEE: Ridiculous.

20 CAITLIN: Are you both done? *(They say nothing.)* We are
21   going to the Greek place because it is across the street
22   from the Mesa. Jen, the Korean place you like is all the
23   way in Orange. And Brittney, the Adam Sandler movie
24   is only playing in Hollywood until next week. So, do you
25   want to drive all that way?

26 BRITTNEY: Fine.

27 JENILEE: So, why can't we go to the Korean Barbeque
28   place?

29 CAITLIN: Because, with the cost of gas now, we have to be
30   smart. You both want to eat out and see a movie, right?
31   *(They both mumble affirmatively.)* OK. Then we go to
32   Huntington Beach to the Greek place, eat the half-price
33   lunch, walk across the street to the Mesa and see *Gone*
34   *with the Wind,* a movie we all love, and then we move
35   on from there.

1 JENILEE: You have the whole day planned, don't you?

2 CAITLIN: Well, duh.

3 BRITTNEY: Why don't you two go and just bring me back

4   ice cream.

5 JENILEE: Ooooh, ice cream. I haven't had ice cream since

6   Saturday.

7 CAITLIN: We are not *bringing* you back ice cream. In fact, if

8   you check out this bulleted list, you will see what I have

9   planned for after the movie.

10 JENILEE: *(Takes the list and groans.)*

11 BRITTNEY: What? *(She takes the list.)*

12 CAITLIN: It will be fun.

13 JENILEE: Yuck.

14 BRITTNEY: No. I'm not going.

15 CAITLIN: Yeah, you are.

16 BRITTNEY: No, I'm not.

17 JENILEE: Why would we go to the gym?

18 CAITLIN: Well, think about it. We eat lunch, we go to see a

19   long movie and eat popcorn and a pound bag of Reese's

20   Pieces, which, if you examine the list, you will see we

21   pick up at Target before we go to the movie. We will

22   need to move around. Come on, think it through.

23 BRITTNEY: I don't want to think it through.

24 JENILEE: We're going to be all the way down in Huntington

25   Beach and drive back and go to the gym? What a drag.

26 CAITLIN: No. We'll go to the gym in Huntington Beach.

27 BRITTNEY: Noooo. I don't want to work out.

28 CAITLIN: Look I've planned this whole thing out.

29 BRITTNEY: Of course you have ...

30 CAITLIN: You'll thank me later.

31 JENILEE: I doubt it.

32 CAITLIN: Look, we all have memberships at Bally's Gym,

33   right?

34 JENILEE: Yeah.

35 BRITTNEY: I think mine expired.

1 CAITLIN: No, it didn't. Your dad paid it.
2 BRITTNEY: What?
3 CAITLIN: He thinks you need to firm up.
4 BRITTNEY: He what?
5 CAITLIN: I was helping him re-organize his file folders on
6   the computer before I came upstairs and he mentioned
7   it.
8 BRITTNEY: He mentioned that I was fat to my friend? What
9   gives?
10 JENILEE: Seriously.
11 CAITLIN: Need firming. Fat was never mentioned.
12 BRITTNEY: And why were you helping him with the
13   computer?
14 CAITLIN: I saw him working on it and his desktop looks
15   like your floor. I just showed him a better way to
16   organize.
17 JENILEE: Can't you leave anyone alone?
18 CAITLIN: He asked me.
19 BRITTNEY: So, my father paid for a gym membership?
20   What does that say? What am I supposed to take from
21   that?
22 CAITLIN: Oh, I don't know. Get off your lazy butt? Just a
23   thought. Now let's get started on the day!
24 JENILEE: I don't feel like it. I'm depressed. Jonathan and I
25   are breaking up.
26 CAITLIN: Again?
27 JENILEE: Yeah. Again. I just don't know what to do.
28 CAITLIN: Oh good grief. You don't even like the guy.
29 JENILEE: What?
30 CAITLIN: You keep him around so you can have something
31   to whine about. Waaaah, Jonathan didn't call me.
32   Waaaah, Jonathan calls too much. Waaaah, Jonathan
33   cheated on me. Waaaah, waaaah, call the
34   waaaahmbulance.
35 JENILEE: Shut up.

1 BRITTNEY: *(Laughing)* **You know it's true. Come on. Admit**
2   **it. You don't even like him anymore. You said so. And**
3   **he's a lousy kisser, you said that, too.**
4 JENILEE: *(Starting to laugh, too)* **He is!!!**
5 CAITLIN: *(Again, whipping out the list)* **So we add Jenilee**
6   **breaks up with Jonathan today to the list. OK?**
7 BRITTNEY: **Works for me.**
8 JENILEE: **Sure, why not? Who cares? I'm tired of him**
9   **anyway.**
10 CAITLIN: **Cool, Brit, got a pen?**
11 BRITTNEY: **Look under the pile of bras in the corner.**
12 CAITLIN: **Never mind, I'll remember.**
13 BRITTNEY: **Suit yourself.**
14 CAITLIN: **So, Lazy gets out of the house, Whiney breaks up**
15   **with Jonathan and ...**
16 JENILEE: **And Demanding finally shuts up!**
17 CAITLIN: **I don't see that happening. If I don't get you two**
18   **going, you'd do nothing all day.**
19 BRITTNEY: **I still don't understand why we have to go the**
20   **gym, much less go to the gym all the way in Huntington**
21   **Beach.**
22 CAITLIN: **I have a plan ...**
23 JENILEE: **Of course you do ...**
24 BRITTNEY: **She always does.**
25 CAITLIN: **What is the date?**
26 BRITTNEY: **May tenth. Exactly one month 'til graduation.**
27 JENILEE: **I don't know if I can last that long.**
28 CAITLIN: **And what happens the weekend of May tenth?**
29   *(They look at her blankly.)* **Hello! Huntington Beach Surf**
30   **Championships. And where are all those surfers**
31   **working out? At Bally's!**
32 BRITTNEY: **Let's go!**
33 JENILEE: **I'm ready.**
34 CAITLIN: **First we have to check off the other things on the**
35   **list.**

1   BRITTNEY: I don't want to clean my room and I'm not
2   going to. I live here, not you. And that's the end of the
3   discussion.
4   CAITLIN: What about lunch and the movie?
5   JENILEE: I'm good with that. But first, I want to move the
6   breaking up with Jonathan thing to the top of the list.
7   If I am going to hook up with some surfer tonight, I
8   should at least break up with Jonathan before that. I
9   wouldn't want to cheat on him. That would be wrong.
10   *(The girls share a nasty smile — no explanation*
11   *necessary.)*
12   CAITLIN: OK, let's get a move on. And a thank you for
13   planning this day would be nice. Jenilee, find the
14   phone and break up with Jonathan. Brit, at least pick
15   up your wet towels. I swear, we'd do nothing but sit on
16   our butts and whine if it weren't for me.
17   BRITTNEY: Yeah, you're a queen.
18   CAITLIN: Yes, I am. Now, up. We have a busy, busy day
19   ahead of us. I'm going down to check on your father
20   and his computer. Jen, I want you broken up with
21   Jonathan by the time I get back. *(As she is leaving)* If I
22   didn't take care of things, nothing would get done.
23   JENILEE: She's so pushy.
24   BRITTNEY: She exhausts me.
25   JENILEE: She's always right, isn't she?
26   BRITTNEY: Yeah. If she weren't one of our best friends, I'd
27   hate her.
28   JENILEE: No kidding. So, where's the phone?
29   BRITTNEY: I don't know. Call it with your cell phone and
30   find it when it rings.
31   JENILEE: God, you're lazy!
32   BRITTNEY: Quit whining!
33   CAITLIN: *(Calling from Off-stage)* Hurry up!
34   BRITTNEY and JENILEE: All right!!!

Five-Minute One-Acts

The Car

Cast: Jon, Jimmy
Setting: Jon and Jimmy's driveway
Props: Set of car keys, wallet, gas can

1 JON: *(Trying to start the car)* **Come on, start. Come on. I'm**
2   **begging you, just start.**
3 JIMMY: *(Who has been watching JON try to start the car)* **Just**
4   **what do you think you are doing?**
5 JON: **Going to a party at David's.**
6 JIMMY: **And how do you think you are getting there?**
7 JON: **Well, Jimmy, by the looks of it, I would guess that I am**
8   **taking your car.**
9 JIMMY: **Jon, I don't know whether or not you noticed this,**
10   **but in your rush to leave, you forgot to do one small**
11   **thing.**
12 JON: **What?** *(He tries the ignition again, which still won't start*
13   *the engine.)* **I cannot believe this. Did you put gas in the**
14   **car today?**
15 JIMMY: **No. I didn't know that it needed gas. When I used it**
16   **yesterday, it had half a tank.**
17 JON: **Oh, well, I guess I ran it down last night. Got any**
18   **money?**
19 JIMMY: **As I was saying, in your rush to leave for your little**
20   **social engagement, perhaps you forgot to ask me if you**
21   **could use my car.**
22 JON: **You weren't around.**
23 JIMMY: *(Reaching in, pulling JON out of the car)* **Well, I'm**
24   **here now, moron. Get out of the stinkin' car.**
25 JON: **What? What's the problem?**

1 JIMMY: I can't believe you. *(He throws Jon to one side, and*
2   *proceeds to shove him on every point.)* **First you take my**
3   **car last night. Then you run out the gas to fumes. Then**
4   **you take it tonight. Without asking! And now, you want**
5   **money for gas.**
6 JON: **What!?! What's wrong?**
7 JIMMY: *(Grabbing the keys from JON)* **It's *my* car, it's *my* gas,**
8   **and it's *my* money.**
9 JON: *(Grabbing the keys back)* **And I'm *your* brother.**
10 JIMMY: **Accident of birth.** *(He takes the keys from JON's*
11   *hand.)*
12 JON: **So, you won't let me use the car?**
13 JIMMY: **You don't miss a trick, do you?** *(He begins to leave as*
14   *JON tries to ask again.)* **Give it up, little brother.**
15 JON: **You are so selfish and inconsiderate. I'd let you use it**
16   **if it were my car.**
17 JIMMY: **The day you get a job and actually use your own**
18   **money to pay for something, we'll talk. Until then, keep**
19   **your greedy little hands *off* of my stuff. Now, get out of**
20   **my way, you little loser.**
21 JON: *(Watching for a moment, makes sure he is gone)* **And he**
22   **calls me a moron.** *(He looks at Jimmy's wallet that he*
23   *took when he grabbed his brother and counts the*
24   *money.)* **Ha, ha, yes indeedy.** *(He goes to the bumper of*
25   *the car and gets spare key.)* **Yes sirree bob.** *(He puts in one*
26   *gallon of lawnmower gas.)* **This should do it.** *(Turns the*
27   *ignition, smiles as car starts.)* **Yes, it's a good life!!**

The Cast List

Cast: Jon, Matt

Setting: School hallway, there is a list posted on the wall.

1   JON: Matt, come on, it's up.

2   MATT: What, you couldn't wait until I parked the car?

3   JON: Maybe if you didn't drive like my grandmother I

4   wouldn't have had to jump out of a rolling car.

5   MATT: Safety first.

6   JON: I swear, you are an old man.

7   MATT: Yeah, great. *(He looks over to the posted cast list.)* **OK,**

8   **ready?**

9   JON: Yes. To be honest, though, I don't even have to look. I

10   know I made the play.

11   MATT: You are such a jerk.

12   JON: Confident.

13   MATT: Jerk. I don't know why you have to be such a fool. If

14   you made it and I didn't, you better keep your mouth

15   shut about it.

16   JON: Ha! I've been waiting for a long time to be in a play.

17   This is a long time coming. I even quit football so I

18   could try out.

19   MATT: You know, it's not that easy to make the plays here.

20   JON: So?

21   MATT: And you really didn't prepare your audition piece.

22   JON: So?

23   MATT: And the director knew it.

24   JON: So? She also knows that I'm talented. That alone

25   should get me in.

26   MATT: I guess so. OK, let's look.

27   JON: OK. *(They walk over together, see it. Both are silent for a*

28   *moment.)* **Huh.**

29   MATT: Huh.

1   JON: You made it. Good. Good. I'm glad.

2   MATT: Thanks. *(Silence while JON studies the list)*

3   JON: Wait a minute. Look, there it says understudy, Jon

4   Roberts. Oh, I get it, she's still thinking about my part

5   in the show, it's "under study."

6   MATT: Uh huh. *(He starts to giggle, then laughs out loud at*

7   *JON's stupidity.)* Moron! Understudy doesn't mean she's

8   thinking about casting you in a part. It means you

9   aren't in the show unless someone gets sick or dies.

10 JON: I'm not in it? I didn't make it? So, fine. No big deal, I'll

11   just go back to football. Who cares, right?

12 MATT: Right. *(They start to walk away, MATT suppressing*

13   *snickers.)* Football's good, too.

14 JON: Yeah. *(A moment passes.)* That witch!! She knows how

15   much this means to me. I can't believe it. Oh my God!

16   *(He goes back to look at the cast list.)* Look at this. Bobby,

17   he's no good. Joey, he can't act right. I'm better than all

18   these people. What's she thinking?

19 MATT: Maybe she's thinking she doesn't want to work with

20   an ass.

21 JON: Personality shouldn't matter. Talent should matter.

22   I'm better than everyone on this frickin' list.

23 MATT: Yeah, well, you may be better, but we're all in it,

24   right? Hey, buddy, walk home.

25 JON: Fine! I'll walk! I don't need you or this stupid play. *(He*

26   *looks again at the list.)* I don't believe it!

The Date

Cast: Eddie, Frank

Setting: Inside Eddie and Frank's house

1   EDDIE: I need to take a shower.
2   FRANK: Well, I guess you're going to have to wait until I'm
3   done.
4   EDDIE: I've been waiting an hour already.
5   FRANK: You're just going to have to wait a little longer,
6   then, aren't you? I'm getting ready for Tammy.
7   EDDIE: You know, big brother, that ever since you have
8   been going out with Tammy all you do is talk about
9   going out with her, get ready to go out with her or
10   actually go out with her.
11 FRANK: I've got the song of love in my heart.
12 EDDIE: Your life is rapidly becoming played on one note.
13 FRANK: You're just jealous that Tammy's my girl.
14 EDDIE: To be perfectly honest, Frank, I've never given her
15   a second thought.
16 FRANK: Are you badmouthing the woman I love?
17 EDDIE: No, I'm not. I am, however, getting really tired of
18   talking about nothing but her and watching you fall
19   into this zombie mode. It's sickening.
20 FRANK: It's love.
21 EDDIE: Whatever. All I want right now, though, is for you to
22   get out of this bathroom so I can get ready for my date.
23 FRANK: Eddie, you have a date?
24 EDDIE: Why do you sound so shocked? Do you think
25   women find me unappealing? I have more than my
26   share of women.
27 FRANK: I've noticed. That's what I meant. Only one date
28   tonight?
29 EDDIE: You sound surprised.

1   FRANK: No, I didn't mean it that way. I just thought that
2   you weren't, you know, interested.
3   EDDIE: I'm not interested in a long-term, whipped kind of
4   thing that you're in. I'm in it for the quick excitement
5   and short run.
6   FRANK: Ah, I see. In other words, you're a pig.
7   EDDIE: You act like it's a bad thing.
8   FRANK: And you think I've got a problem because I'm with
9   one girl? You're the one with the problem.
10   EDDIE: No, I'm the one with the *women*. You're the one
11   with the *woman*. It's a matter of singular versus plural.
12   I happen to like my fun in quantity.
13   FRANK: Well, I'm in it for the quality. I feel sorry for you.
14   You're missing a lot.
15   EDDIE: Funny, I was just about to say the same thing to you.
16   FRANK: Well, I'm off to my girlfriend. You have a great time
17   with whoever it is you'll waste your life with tonight.
18   EDDIE: Ah, one man's waste is another man's feast. I plan
19   on dining well tonight. *(Both laugh and exit.)*

Facing the Enemy

Cast: Rick, Sam

Setting: A hallway at school

1 RICK: The movie is at three-thirty, OK?

2 SAM: What movie?

3 RICK: Sam, I told you that we were going to meet Debbie
4   and Leah today at the show.

5 SAM: Today? Was that today?

6 RICK: Yes, it was today. What's the matter with you? You
7   never listen to anything I say.

8 SAM: Rick, I can't go.

9 RICK: Oh, no you don't. You're not leaving me alone to face
10   those girls. You promised that this time you'd go.

11 SAM: I can't. What will I say? How will I act?

12 RICK: Just be yourself.

13 SAM: Oh, great. Look how well that's worked for me in the
14   past. Girls hate me.

15 RICK: They don't hate you. They're just a little
16   uncomfortable around a guy who never says anything
17   except "excuse me."

18 SAM: That's because I am always doing stupid things. I am
19   constantly excusing myself. I'm an embarrassment.
20   Why did you ask them to meet us?

21 RICK: Listen to me. Leah said she thinks you're cute.

22 SAM: No way!

23 RICK: I swear. She said she really wants to get together with
24   you.

25 SAM: With me? Get together with me? What will I do? How
26   do I act? What do I say?

27 RICK: Just be cool, be natural. Be like me.

28 SAM: Like you? You mean talk to her? And try to touch her?

29 RICK: Well, I'm not saying throw her on the ground and

1 climb on top. What I am saying is that you're a man,
2 and she's a woman. Take it from there.
3 SAM: I'm a man and she's a woman. I never thought of it
4 that way. That makes it a little clearer, doesn't it?
5 RICK: All you have to remember is that you're the man.
6 You're the one in charge. Assert yourself. Let her know
7 that you're in command of affairs at hand.
8 SAM: Affairs at hand? You didn't say anything about an
9 affair being at hand. Oh, gosh, I think I'm going to be
10 sick.
11 RICK: Sam, Samster, pal. Just remember, she's probably as
12 nervous as you, maybe more so. After all, she's the one
13 who wanted to meet you. This was her idea.
14 SAM: It was?
15 RICK: Yeah. She's really interested. *(Taking him by the*
16 *shoulders)* Now, stand proud. Be a man. Pull yourself
17 together, and let's go out and divide and conquer.
18 SAM: Divide and conquer. Real men. I'm in charge. I am the
19 man.
20 RICK: Good! Now you've got it. Onward to face the enemy.
21 SAM: Onward! *(He stops.)* Just a minute.
22 RICK: What now?
23 SAM: I've got to throw up. Wait here.

The Fight

Cast: Josh, Rick, Matt

Setting: Outside, perhaps in an empty parking lot

1 JOSH: *(Pacing nervously, he looks around, clearly waiting for*
2   *someone to come.)* **Where is he? Darn it.** *(Finally, he sees*
3   *someone approaching.)* **Awesome! Rick! Over here!**
4 RICK: **You're an idiot.**
5 JOSH: **Yeah, I know. Thanks for coming.**
6 RICK: **One of these days I'm not going to be able to make it**
7   **to save your butt, then what are you going to do?**
8 JOSH: **It'll never happen. You're my best friend. It's your**
9   **obligation. You know I'd do the same for you.**
10 RICK: **Yeah, that'll happen. I can fight my own battles.**
11 JOSH: **But, if you ever need backup, I'm there. You can**
12   **count on it.**
13 RICK: **Yeah, great. So, where is this guy?**
14 JOSH: **He said he'd be here tonight at eleven o'clock. It's ten**
15   **after. Maybe he's not coming.**
16 RICK: **Shauna's waiting for me to come over to take her to**
17   **Tom's party. You've got five more minutes for this guy**
18   **to show up, then we're out of here.**
19 JOSH: **No problem. I came. My pride is intact.**
20 RICK: **How do you get yourself into these messes?**
21 JOSH: **I didn't know the girl had a boyfriend.**
22 RICK: **You will hit on anything that doesn't move, won't**
23   **you?**
24 JOSH: **I like women.** *(He hears something.)* **Look over there.**
25   **Yeah, that's him.**
26 RICK: **OK, lets make this fast.** *(He looks.)*
27 MATT: *(Walking right over to JOSH)* **Punk.**
28 JOSH: **Loser.**
29 RICK: **Matt?**

1 MATT: *(Turning and seeing RICK)* **Rick?**
2 RICK: *(Surprised to see it's MATT)* **Hey, buddy!**
3 MATT: **Hey! Howya doing?**
4 RICK: **Great. Great. Saw you at the last game. Excellent**
5   **pass.**
6 MATT: **Thanks. Yeah, the team did great this year. How's**
7   **wrestling so far?**
8 RICK: **Doing good.**
9 MATT: **I saw that write up in the paper about you.**
10   **Impressive. Undefeated this year, huh?**
11 RICK: **Yeah, yeah. Kinda cool. You got Mrs. Margraff for**
12   **Chem?**
13 MATT: **First period. Tough!**
14 RICK: **She's no easier fifth period.**
15 MATT: **You going to Tom's party tonight?**
16 RICK: **Yeah, after this.**
17 JOSH: **Hello!**
18 MATT: **Oh ... you're here with him?**
19 RICK: **So, you're the guy that wants to fight Josh?**
20 MATT: **Yeah. Little punk hit on my girl.**
21 RICK: **Yeah, he does that a lot. He doesn't mean anything by**
22   **it.**
23 MATT: **How do you know him?**
24 RICK: **Our families have been friends forever. He's like my**
25   **little brother.**
26 MATT: **That's a shame. I'm gonna have to pound him.**
27 RICK: **Hmmm. Well, I'm afraid I can't let you do that.**
28 MATT: **What? He hit on Paige. You know we've been going**
29   **out since May. She's my girl.**
30 JOSH: **What? Did you put your mark on her?**
31 RICK: **Shutting up about now would be good, Josh.**
32 JOSH: **Sorry ...**
33 RICK: **Josh, did you not know that she had a boyfriend?**
34 JOSH: **I told you, I didn't. She didn't act like she did.**
35 MATT: **What did she do?**

1   JOSH: She flirted with me. She smiled.

2   MATT: So you kiss her?

3   JOSH: No! *(RICK gives him a look.)* **OK, maybe. But she**

4   **didn't kiss back, so I backed off. That was it.**

5   MATT: Time to throw down.

6   RICK: Matt, I don't think so.

7   MATT: This isn't your business, Rick.

8   RICK: I'm making it my business. You and I are friends

9   from school, but Josh is like family. You're going to

10   have to go through me to get to him. That's just the way

11   it is.

12 MATT: I'm not here to fight you.

13 RICK: I don't want to fight, either. Shauna is waiting for me

14   to take her to Tom's party. Josh is an idiot, but he's

15   harmless.

16 JOSH: That's true ... wait a minute ...

17 RICK: He hit on your girl, she didn't respond, he backed off,

18   end of story. Now, if you want to make more of this, we

19   can. But, I repeat: You will have to go through me to get

20   to him, and I think we both know how that will end up.

21 MATT: *(He evaluates the situation.)* **Whatever, dude. You**

22   **know I respect you, so it ends.** *(To JOSH)* **For now. But**

23   **you better stay away from Paige.**

24 JOSH: No problem.

25 MATT: And maybe you better investigate a situation before

26   you start putting your lips on a girl you don't know.

27 RICK: I've been telling him that since he hit puberty.

28 JOSH: I can't help myself.

29 MATT: Well, you better learn. Because next time, maybe the

30   guy won't respect your backup guy.

31 RICK: *(Holding out his hand)* **Thanks, Matt.**

32 MATT: *(Shaking his hand)* **Not a problem.** *(To JOSH)* **See you**

33   **around, punk.** *(Exits.)*

34 RICK: *(Smacking JOSH on the head)* **Idiot.**

35 JOSH: I know. So, we going to Tom's party?

1   RICK: Can you keep yourself focused on just girls you
2   know?
3   JOSH: I'll do my best.
4   RICK: Loser. Let's go.
5   JOSH: Hey, Rick. Thanks.
6   RICK: Yeah, yeah. *(They exit.)*

Heather

Cast: Alex, Dylan
Setting: The school hallway

1   ALEX: Dylan ... Hey, Dylan, wait up.

2   DYLAN: I've got to get to class.

3   ALEX: Yeah, I know. I'm in the same class as you.

4   DYLAN: Uh ... I have to stop by my locker. I might be late to
5   class.

6   ALEX: OK. If we're both a little late, maybe Mr. Garcia will
7   spread the anger and not focus it on just one of us.

8   DYLAN: Oh ... yeah. Well, to be honest, I might not even go
9   to class, so why don't you just head on over without me.

10 ALEX: What?

11 DYLAN: I mean I will probably go, but I might not, so don't
12   wait on me.

13 ALEX: What is your problem lately, buddy?

14 DYLAN: I don't know what you mean.

15 ALEX: Well, I call you up to go bowling and you're busy. I
16   call you up to go clubbing and you say you're grounded.
17   I call you to just hang out and you say you have
18   homework. What's the deal?

19 DYLAN: Nothing, Alex. I'm just busy lately.

20 ALEX: Too busy for your friends?

21 DYLAN: No.

22 ALEX: Oh. Just too busy for me?

23 DYLAN: Uh ... well ...

24 ALEX: What's the problem?

25 DYLAN: Nothing.

26 ALEX: Don't do your usual passive/aggressive thing with
27   me. We've known each other too long. Just say what's
28   on your mind.

29 DYLAN: It's nothing, honest.

1   ALEX: OK ... so, after class you want to go to Mickey D's and
2   get something to eat?
3   DYLAN: Sorry, I'm busy ...
4   ALEX: *(Saying it with him)* ... busy.
5   DYLAN: Yeah. I am. Really.
6   ALEX: Doing ...?
7   DYLAN: I'm going out with Heather.
8   ALEX: Really? That's great! Finally asked her out, huh?
9   DYLAN: Yeah.
10   ALEX: Took you long enough. I thought you'd never get
11   around to it.
12   DYLAN: Well, there was something in my way.
13   ALEX: What?
14   DYLAN: You.
15   ALEX: Me? What?
16   DYLAN: You, buddy. You're always flirting with her.
17   ALEX: I flirt with everybody.
18   DYLAN: But you knew I liked her.
19   ALEX: And you knew I didn't. I was just flirting and having
20   fun.
21   DYLAN: But you knew that I wanted to ask her out.
22   ALEX: No one was stopping you.
23   DYLAN: Alex! You know how hard it is to talk to a girl when
24   she's giggling with you? I told you I liked her, you
25   should have backed off. Heather was mine.
26   ALEX: What?! Yours?! Why?
27   DYLAN: Forget it.
28   ALEX: That's what I mean by your passive/aggressive thing.
29   Buddy, if you wanted her, she was there for the taking.
30   I never liked her that way, and you knew it. Don't
31   blame your lack of moves on me, my friend.
32   DYLAN: You were in the way.
33   ALEX: All I did was talk to her. Jeez, Dylan, get a
34   testosterone injection, be a man. If you like a girl, then
35   go for it and don't blame other people if you lose out

1   from waiting too long.

2 DYLAN: Well, I did ask her out! And she said yes!

3 ALEX: Of course she did. She likes you. Everyone knows

4   that.

5 DYLAN: Not me.

6 ALEX: You would if you weren't such a wuss.

7 DYLAN: Thanks.

8 ALEX: It's true. I mean, girls like the shy thing, but don't let

9   it hold you back. Make your move, go for it. Heather

10   likes you, she told me.

11 DYLAN: She did?

12 ALEX: Yeah. Right in the middle of my harmless flirting.

13 DYLAN: Hmm. OK, but from now on, you stop the flirting

14   with her.

15 ALEX: Whatever, man. If it will make you feel better.

16 DYLAN: It will. She really likes me, huh?

17 ALEX: She must if she could resist my many charms.

18 DYLAN: Yeah ... right. So, where should I take her after

19   school?

20 ALEX: Feed her.

21 DYLAN: Food. Good idea. That way I won't have to talk

22   'cause my mouth will be full.

23 ALEX: You want me to come and keep the conversation

24   going? *(DYLAN gives him a look.)* **Perhaps not.**

25 DYLAN: *(Sing-song)* **I'm going out with Heather today!!**

26   *(They exit.)*

Lost in the Desert

Cast: Matt, Jon

Setting: Walking through the desert

Props: A map, a water bottle

1 MATT: Check the map again.

2 JON: I'm telling you, we should have turned left at that big

3   rock.

4 MATT: We did turn left at the big rock.

5 JON: The first big rock, not the second big rock.

6 MATT: There are thousands of big rocks out here. There is

7   no first or second big rock. They are all big giant rocks

8   that have no numbers. Do you see numbers on any of

9   these rocks?

10 JON: I meant the big rock that had that jagged edge. You

11   know which one I meant. It was about a mile back.

12 MATT: Oh, sure, the jagged edge. Now I remember. It was

13   next to the one with the other jagged edge. Next to the

14   other big rock, the first one, not the second one. Now I

15   see what you mean.

16 JON: Sarcasm isn't going to help us. Do you have any water

17   left?

18 MATT: No, I finished back at the big rock with the jagged

19   edge.

20 JON: You drank all of the water? Jeez.

21 MATT: Listen, it's at least one hundred twenty degrees out

22   here, no shade, we've been walking in this desert for

23   hours because you thought a hike in the morning

24   would be invigorating. And now we are lost.

25 JON: Don't exaggerate. We've been walking for only about

26   an hour. Look around you. Enjoy all of God's majesty in

27   creation. You've got to wonder how all of this miracle

28   occurs. Look at these rocks, these mountains, the great

29   open sky. How? How is this all possible?

1 MATT: Well, buddy, we will be meeting up with God pretty
2   darn soon if we don't find our way back to civilization.
3   You can ask him yourself how he created the heavens
4   and the earth.
5 JON: Stop complaining, you big wuss.
6 MATT: We're lost, buddy. Lost in the desert. We're miles
7   from civilization. The temperature is only going to get
8   hotter and we're out of water.
9 JON: You are so negative. We're only about an hour's walk
10   from camp.
11 MATT: In the heat of hell.
12 JON: A good sweat will do you good.
13 MATT: We have no water.
14 JON: Look over there, to the right.
15 MATT: What? What's there?
16 JON: For God's sake, man, look. It's a lake.
17 MATT: Jon. There are no lakes in the desert.
18 JON: You've never heard of Lake Mojave?
19 MATT: Yeah, in Nevada. We're in California, forty miles
20   outside of Barstow.
21 JON: Matt, look in the sky. Birds. Where there are birds,
22   there is water.
23 MATT: Those are buzzards, my friend. Where there are
24   buzzards, there are the carcasses of the dead. And if
25   you look closely, they are starting to circle us. They
26   know dinner when they see it.
27 JON: OK. Let's start walking. Buzzards won't go after a
28   moving target. As long as we are moving, then we are
29   not dead.
30 MATT: Oh, we're dead, all right. The buzzards know.
31   They're smart birds. They can smell death.
32 JON: Just shut up and keep moving. *(Shouting up to the*
33   *birds)* Back off, bird-boys. We're not dinner yet.
34 MATT: Walk, Jon. Don't antagonize them. Just keep
35   walking.

Priorities

Cast: Zachary, Tyler

Setting: An empty room

1   ZACHARY: Tyler, what are you doing in here?

2   TYLER: I just need to get away for a while.

3   ZACHARY: You OK?

4   TYLER: Fine, Zach. I'm fine.

5   ZACHARY: OK. *(A pause)* You going to stay in here much

6   longer?

7   TYLER: I don't know. Just give me a minute or two.

8   ZACHARY: Buddy, the party's out there. You're bringing us

9   down.

10 TYLER: Sorry. I just need some time.

11 ZACHARY: For what?

12 TYLER: For nothing. For thinking. I don't know. Just some

13   time.

14 ZACHARY: Is this really the occasion for that?

15 TYLER: It is for me. Judy's here.

16 ZACHARY: Oh brother. So?

17 TYLER: She's here with Ryan.

18 ZACHARY: That's because they are going together.

19 TYLER: Well, she used to go with me.

20 ZACHARY: You broke up with her.

21 TYLER: It was a mistake.

22 ZACHARY: You should have thought of that when you were

23   cheating on her.

24 TYLER: I didn't know what I had.

25 ZACHARY: Well, this whole thing is your fault.

26 TYLER: I know that. And thanks for pointing it out again.

27   Appreciate it.

28 ZACHARY: So, you're going to stay in here having your own

29   little pity party?

1   TYLER: Shut up, Zachary.
2   ZACHARY: Hey, this is my birthday and my party. This is a
3   great gift, your mood. I'd like to thank you for that.
4   TYLER: This isn't about you. I lost the one girl I've ever
5   loved.
6   ZACHARY: Loved? You're sixteen years old. Get off it. Now
7   come on. Quit being a big drag.
8   TYLER: I did love her.
9   ZACHARY: You loved the idea of her.
10 TYLER: Nope.
11 ZACHARY: So, you loved having to call her at least once a
12   day? You loved getting her little notes in your locker?
13   You loved having to eat lunch with her every day? You
14   loved her text messages telling where and when to
15   meet her after school? You loved having to sit with her
16   at games rather than with your friends?
17 TYLER: She cared.
18 ZACHARY: She smothered.
19 TYLER: I miss that.
20 ZACHARY: *(Quickly)* Gun to your head and choose. Your car
21   and Judy fall off a cliff. Which would you miss the
22   most? *(Points finger at TYLER's head like a gun.)*
23 TYLER: *(Quickly)* My car. *(Surprised)* Huh. How about that?
24   Wow. Am I really that shallow?
25 ZACHARY: Yes, yes you are. Now you go out to the party and
26   dance and hook up with some little hottie and have a
27   great time. It's what adolescence is all about.
28 TYLER: And I'll make sure that Judy sees me. *(He exits*
29   *happily.)*
30 ZACHARY: Grow up!

Trek

Cast: Jordan, Jim
Setting: In front of a TV

1　JORDAN: *(Playing a video game)* **Yes!!**

2　JIM: **Jordan, are you still playing with that stupid game?**

3　JORDAN: **Yes, Jim.** *(To the game)* **Phasers on full. *Fire!!***

4　JIM: **Listen to me. You spend entirely too much time**
5　　**playing with those dumb games. You need a life, and**
6　　**you need one today.**

7　JORDAN: **Jim, you're the captain. You have to decide the**
8　　**right course.**

9　JIM: **I am not a captain. I'm your brother. Put away that**
10　　**darn Star Trek game and let's go out and find a woman.**

11　JORDAN: **Ah, Jim, you always were the one with the ladies,**
12　　**weren't you?**

13　JIM: **Let's go. Do you want to spend your entire life in front**
14　　**of a TV set playing video games?**

15　JORDAN: **I am willing to go where no man has gone before.**
16　　**I accept your mission.**

17　JIM: **Does that mean you want to come with us?**

18　JORDAN: **Will the Klingons be there? I've never trusted the**
19　　**Klingons, you know.**

20　JIM: **Idiot. No Klingons, but Matt and the gang. And let's**
21　　**leave the funny Trek stuff at home, OK?**

22　JORDAN: **Funny stuff? Jim, I'm a doctor, not a comedian.**

23　JIM: **You're a fifteen-year-old fanatic.**

24　JORDAN: **Can thirty-five thousand Trekkies be wrong?**

25　JIM: **Trekkie is one thing. Obsession is another. Now, knock**
26　　**it off and let's go.**

27　JORDAN: **OK, fine. Beam us up, Scotty.**

28　JIM: *(Grabbing him)* **There is no Scotty. There is no beaming.**
29　　**Jordan, I am getting really worried about you.**

1   JORDAN: Worried? That is illogical. I am fine.

2   JIM: All you do is talk about Star Trek. I keep waiting for

3   your ears to suddenly turn into points.

4   JORDAN: Also illogical. Humanoids do not have pointy

5   ears. Only Vulcans.

6   JIM: That's it. I'm getting in the car and leaving your

7   warped little mind at home.

8   JORDAN: Engage at warp five.

9   JIM: Engage this, Jordan. I'm talking to Mom about this,

10   and telling her that I think all this video stuff has got to

11   go. It's getting to be too much.

12   JORDAN: Each man has his own trial by fire he must

13   survive. I wish you well in your efforts.

14   JIM: Snap out of it, kid. Come back to Earth.

15   JORDAN: Jim. I'm just having fun. Have you forgotten what

16   it's like to be a kid and have fun? Loosen up.

17   JIM: Turn it off, Jordy, and let's go.

18   JORDAN: You sure you want me with you?

19   JIM: You're my brother. And I promise that together, we

20   shall live long and prosper.

21   JORDAN: Then let's make it so. *(Looking up at him)* You're

22   OK, you know? You're OK. *(They exit.)*

Ten-Minute One-Acts

The Poker Game

Cast: Brandon, David, Shane, Adam
Setting: A poker game at David's house
Props: Tray with assorted food and drinks,
poker chips and deck of cards

1 BRANDON: David, you got anything to drink?

2 DAVID: Yeah ...

3 SHANE: Food?

4 DAVID: Yeah ... gimme a second ...

5 ADAM: You knew we were coming here, why isn't the food

6   ready?

7 BRANDON: What's poker without food?

8 DAVID: *(Entering with tray of food and drinks)* It would be

9   poker at your house, loser.

10 BRANDON: I resent that!

11 ADAM: No, you resemble that ...

12 SHANE: You never have food at your house.

13 BRANDON: I can't help it. And, Shane, you never even have

14   the game at your house.

15 SHANE: My parents don't approve of gambling under their

16   roof.

17 DAVID: But it's OK under someone else's roof?

18 SHANE: Go figure. Adam, toss me one of those Cokes.

19 ADAM: Diet or regular?

20 SHANE: Look at me, buddy. Note the toned arms and flat

21   abs. The diet. Regular!! Please, you insult me.

22 DAVID: So, Brandon, deal.

23 BRANDON: Ante up, my friends. Texas Hold 'em, nothing

24   wild except us! *(He deals and the game continues*

1   *throughout the rest of the scene unless someone folds*
2   *and moves away from the table.)*
3   **ADAM: Yeah, we're a wild group. Friday night, poker with**
4   **the boys, sandwiches prepared by David's mom, who is**
5   **in the other room and sodas. Whoooohoooo, watch out**
6   **for us!**
7   **SHANE: Where's Natasha tonight, Adam?**
8   **ADAM: Church.**
9   **DAVID: Repenting for the sins of going out with you?**
10   **ADAM: She's a good girl.**
11   **BRANDON: So, why's she going out with you?**
12   **ADAM: I'm a catch, buddy! I got it all.**
13   **DAVID: They have medication for that now.**
14   **ADAM: You're a riot, David. Maybe that's why you don't**
15   **have a girlfriend.**
16   **DAVID: Don't want one.** *(Referring to his hand)* **I'm all in.**
17   **SHANE: I got nothing.** *(Tosses his cards in, moves away from*
18   *table.)*
19   **ADAM: Why don't you want one?** *(To his hand)* **I'll call.**
20   **BRANDON: I got nothing.** *(Flips cards to continue game.)*
21   **DAVID: I'm too busy.**
22   **SHANE: With what?**
23   **DAVID: School, ASB, baseball, ya know.**
24   **BRANDON: And you can't fit a woman in all that?**
25   **DAVID: Could, but don't want to.**
26   **BRANDON: This is the river card.**
27   **ADAM: Gimme what I need, baby.**
28   **DAVID:** *(The card is flipped.)* **And there it is!** *(He scoops up*
29   *the pot.)*
30   **SHANE: What's he got?**
31   **ADAM: He gets a two on the river. Oh my God! I have a pair**
32   **of aces and this guy wins with two in the hold and a flip**
33   **of a three.**
34   **SHANE: You are so freakin' lucky.**
35   **DAVID: Skill my friend, skill.**

1 BRANDON: Everyone in?
2 ALL: Yeah, sure, I got some money left. *(Etc.)*
3 BRANDON: Ante up, losers. *(He deals, the game continues.)*
4   OK, I know why I don't have a girlfriend. I can be kind
5   of a jerk.
6 ALL: *(Filled with sarcasm)* No, not really. Come on. You?
7   Never!
8 BRANDON: It's been known to happen. And Shane here, he
9   has plenty of women.
10 SHANE: This is true. Women love me. It's a burden I bear.
11 ADAM: I have a girlfriend.
12 SHANE: Which is proof that there is a merciful God who
13   takes pity on the scum ...
14 ADAM: Say what you will, Natasha will be calling me when
15   she's done with her church thing and then tomorrow
16   we go out.
17 DAVID: And that's the answer.
18 ADAM: What?
19 DAVID: Your life is planned. She calls after church, you go
20   out on Saturday, blah blah blah.
21 SHANE: I don't do that.
22 DAVID: No, you're even worse. You go out with a bunch of
23   different girls, and you have to either lie to them or tell
24   them the truth, then they get all hurt. Too much
25   trouble.
26 BRANDON: I'd like that kind of trouble.
27 DAVID: And you, Brandon, you're the worst. Flip the next
28   card, buddy.
29 BRANDON: Sorry. Who's in?
30 SHANE: Check.
31 ADAM: Raise three.
32 BRANDON: Too rich for me *(He starts to fold, then*
33   *reconsiders.)* Ah, go for it. Why am I the worst?
34 DAVID: Call. 'Cause you want a girl so bad you make a fool
35   of yourself in front of them. It's embarrassing.

1   SHANE: True that.

2   ADAM: Yeah.

3   BRANDON: *(Shrugging)* Yeah, well, waddahya gonna do?

4   DAVID: So, I do the smartest thing.

5   ADAM: Which is?

6   DAVID: Let the ladies come to me. Last card, please.

7   SHANE: Man! Now he flips a queen.

8   ADAM: Nothing!

9   DAVID: Straight. *(He tosses BRANDON a chip.)* A little
10   something for the dealer.

11 SHANE: The ladies come to me.

12 DAVID: They come to you, Shane, because they think they
13   might end up in a "relationship."

14 SHANE: They might.

15 BRANDON: Right. You couldn't stay with one girl longer
16   than a month if your life depended on it.

17 SHANE: Yes, I could.

18 ADAM: When? When have you ever been with one girl
19   longer than it took between haircuts?

20 SHANE: Whatever.

21 ADAM: While I, on the other hand, have the security of a
22   woman who loves me and cares about me ...

23 DAVID: And plans every minute of your life.

24 ADAM: She does not.

25 DAVID: You going to that dance next month?

26 ADAM: Of course.

27 DAVID: *(Mimicking him)* Of course. *(Normal voice)* I'm in.

28 BRANDON: Me, too.

29 SHANE: Raise five.

30 ADAM: Five? You never raise more than two.

31 SHANE: *(He smiles.)* You in or out?

32 ADAM: Out.

33 DAVID and BRANDON: Call. *(The game continues.)*

34 ADAM: So, I'm going to the dance, so what? Of course I'd be
35   going.

1 DAVID: Shane, you?
2 SHANE: Yeah. Don't know with who yet, though. Shirley or
3   Jen.
4 DAVID: Have you told either one yet?
5 SHANE: Nah. The dance is three weeks away. No rush.
6 DAVID: So, they're both waiting on you? Both have probably
7   already turned down other guys hoping you'll ask
8   them.
9 BRANDON: Is that why Kate turned me down? She's
10   waiting for Shane to ask her?
11 ADAM: Yeah, Brandon. You tell yourself that.
12 DAVID: You know something? I've gone to every dance
13   since my sophomore year. Every one.
14 ADAM: Big deal. So have I.
15 DAVID: With Natasha.
16 SHANE: Well, I've gone, too.
17 DAVID: With drama around every one. *(Mimicking*
18   *distraught girls)* Oh, Shane said he'd take me. No me. No
19   me! Shane!!! What's going on? Boo hoo hoo.
20 ADAM: Remember when Britney and Paige got into that
21   fight in the quad and then you turned around and
22   asked Debbie?
23 SHANE: They both got suspended and couldn't go to the
24   dance anyway. Saved me some trouble. I wanted to ask
25   Debbie in the first place.
26 BRANDON: Why didn't you just tell them?
27 SHANE: That would have hurt their feelings.
28 DAVID: And getting in a fight and getting suspended was
29   better?
30 SHANE: At least I didn't look bad.
31 DAVID: You're a sensitive guy, Shane. A real role model.
32 BRANDON: I've gone to dances.
33 DAVID: To every dance? Since your sophomore year?
34 BRANDON: Well, this year. I'm a late bloomer.
35 SHANE: OK, you live in that world, Brandon.

1   DAVID: My point being, *(He looks at the cards and smiles.)* I
2   win again.
3   ADAM, SHANE and BRANDON: I don't believe this! You are
4   so lucky. I hate this game.
5   ADAM: So, what's your point?
6   DAVID: I've never asked a girl to a dance. They always ask
7   me. I'm a nice guy, people like me, I get along with
8   everyone and the girls know that we will be going "as
9   friends." Which, may I add, is financially wise as well.
10   The girl asks, she pays half. It's all good.
11 SHANE: The girl pays? I'm liking that.
12 ADAM: I always have to pay.
13 DAVID: That's because you're a couple. Deadly. And costly.
14 BRANDON: OK, but why don't the girls ask me?
15 DAVID: Because you reek of desperation. It hangs on you
16   like the stench from a freshly fertilized field.
17 ADAM: Nice alliteration.
18 DAVID: You liking that?
19 ADAM: Very nice.
20 DAVID: "A" in English last semester.
21 BRANDON: Hello! You were saying.
22 DAVID: Women are very much like poker.
23 BRANDON: I'm listening.
24 SHANE: Maybe you should be taking notes.
25 BRANDON: Shut up, Shane.
26 SHANE: Merely a suggestion.
27 ADAM: I'd take notes if I were you.
28 DAVID: OK. It's this way. The reason why you never win at
29   poker and you never win with the ladies is because you
30   are always chasing them.
31 BRANDON: Women want to be chased.
32 SHANE: Chased, maybe. Stalked? Whole different thing.
33 DAVID: Seriously. No matter what cards you are holding,
34   you stay in the game. Even if there's no chance of you
35   winning the hand.

1 ADAM: That is so the way you are, Brandon! You never win
2   at poker and you never win with women.
3 DAVID: You gotta know when to hold them and know when
4   to fold them. *(He throws more chips on the table,*
5   *Brandon matches his bet, the rest fold.)*
6 SHANE: Yeah! Like asking Kate to the dance. So out of your
7   league. But then there's Mindy. She'd be all over going
8   with you.
9 BRANDON: But she's not hot.
10 DAVID: Yeah, she is. OK, maybe she's not Kate hot, but she's
11   cute. And really nice. *(The river card is turned.)* She's not
12   a royal flush, but she's a winning hand. Very much like
13   this pair of tens with the ace high. Sorry guys. *(He*
14   *smiles happily and cleans up another pot while the guys*
15   *react loudly and with annoyance.)*
16 BRANDON: I had tens!
17 DAVID: But no ace high. That's a real shame, buddy. And
18   that's what I mean. You go after something you have no
19   way of getting.
20 BRANDON: But we both had tens. Both of us!
21 DAVID: But did you have the ace? No, my young friend, you
22   did not. And that's where we differ. Mindy is your ace,
23   and you're folding.
24 SHANE: Very good analogy, David.
25 ADAM: You deserved that "A," for sure.
26 BRANDON: So I should ask Mindy.
27 DAVID: If you want to go to the dance.
28 BRANDON: *(Getting up)* I'm out. Adam, you deal this one.
29   I'm calling Mindy and locking this in now.
30 SHANE: Excellent move, Brandon, excellent. *(BRANDON*
31   *exits.)*
32 ADAM: You set him up, didn't you? She's going to turn him
33   down.
34 DAVID: That would be funny, wouldn't it? But, no. However,
35   I did ask her if she'd go with him. She said she would.

1   She already has her dress, so what the heck, right?

2   SHANE: So, we're all going to the dance?

3   ADAM: Like I have a choice.

4   DAVID: Who are you taking?

5   SHANE: I don't know, but I know I'm going. I'll figure it out

6   later.

7   ADAM: David, what about you?

8   DAVID: Yeah, probably. Leanne said that Jessica was going

9   to ask me, so whatever.

10   BRANDON: *(Entering)* I have a date! She said yes.

11   DAVID: Excellent work.

12   ADAM: I'm proud of you, man!

13   SHANE: Now deal.

14   BRANDON: OK, I can feel my luck turning. Ante up and

15   prepare to lose all your money. *(He deals quickly.)*

16   DAVID: *(Looking at cards)* I fold.

17   ADAM: *(Looking at cards)* Me, too.

18   SHANE: *(Looking at cards)* I'm out.

19   BRANDON: I won! Did you see that? I won! *(The others shake*

20   *their heads and shrug their shoulders at his joy.)* Hey, I'll

21   take what I can get. *(He smiles and gathers his chips.)*

Right or Wrong

Cast: James, Tyler, Ethan
Setting: Inside James' house
Prop: Phone

1 JAMES: Where is Shane? That boy is never on time.
2 TYLER: He's probably sitting in his room waiting for
3   permission to leave the bed.
4 ETHAN: Lighten up, Tyler.
5 TYLER: I'm just saying ...
6 JAMES: Saying what? You're always making fun of him.
7   He's a good guy. Just a little bit under the parental
8   thumb.
9 TYLER: Not just the parental. He's like a target.
10 ETHAN: Tyler's right, James. He does kind of set himself
11   up. Timid.
12 TYLER: Good word. He's timid. People don't like timidity.
13 JAMES: Well, that's what we're here for.
14 TYLER: Say what?
15 JAMES: To help him out. People know that if they mess
16   with Shane, they mess with us.
17 ETHAN: True, that.
18 TYLER: Sure. Whatever.
19 JAMES: You know you'd back him up, Tyler. Don't deny it.
20 TYLER: I neither deny nor do I admit. I am on a wait and
21   see basis.
22 JAMES: You'd be there in a pinch. We all would.
23 ETHAN: Yeah, I'd back him up. But wait much longer for
24   him? Now that is asking too much.
25 TYLER: The game has already started. We missed the
26   opening kickoff. James, call him and tell him to get his
27   butt over here.
28 ETHAN: What do you want to bet he can't get the car and we

1   have to pick him up.

2   JAMES: Hey, just because we all have cars doesn't mean

3   everyone does. He can't afford it.

4   TYLER: Boo hoo. Call him.

5   JAMES: 'K. *(He dials.)* It's ringing.

6   ETHAN: If the machine answers, hang up and let's just go.

7   JAMES: Very nice, Ethan. *(The phone is answered.)* Hello?

8   Hi, Mrs. Schuster. May I speak to Shane, please ...

9   TYLER: *(Mocking)* "May I speak to Shane, please?"

10   JAMES: *(Whispered)* **Shut up!** *(Into phone)* **Hey, Shane!**

11   Where are you? We've been waiting ... what? *(Alarmed)*

12   What?!

13 ETHAN: What's going on?

14 JAMES: *(Motioning him to be still)* This afternoon? Who?

15   Steven and Jack? Micah, too? Well, first, are you OK?

16   You're sure? OK. You wait right there, we'll be right

17   over. Maybe you should listen to your mom. Don't

18   worry, we'll take care of this. This is what friends are

19   for. *(Hanging up)* Jeez. OK guys, let's go.

20 ETHAN: What happened?

21 TYLER: Where are we going?

22 JAMES: Shane got jumped this afternoon. Steven, Jack and

23   Micah. Three on one.

24 ETHAN: What? How ... ?

25 TYLER: Ouch!

26 JAMES: Apparently they had nothing else to do on a sunny

27   afternoon and decided that instead of going to the

28   mall, they'd jump someone who couldn't fight back.

29   Well, now they'll have to deal with the consequences.

30 TYLER: I'm sorry, what?

31 JAMES: We're going to find those guys and teach them a

32   lesson. Shane is our friend and friends stick together.

33   Right ... ? *(ETHAN and TYLER exchange a look.)* Right?

34 ETHAN: Are you sure Shane didn't provoke this?

35 JAMES: What?

1   ETHAN: You know how he can be sometimes ...
2   JAMES: I do not believe you are saying this. Any way you cut
3   it, three against one isn't fair. Now, let's go.
4   TYLER: Fight?
5   JAMES: Yeah, fight!
6   TYLER: For what?
7   JAMES: Because sometimes you have to meet force with
8   force.
9   TYLER: And sometimes you can just talk it out.
10 JAMES: Shane is at home, bleeding, bruised and battered.
11   His mom said she is going to take him to the hospital
12   because she thinks his ribs are broken. They stomped
13   on his glasses and took his money. The guy's afraid to
14   leave the house because of this and you want to talk it
15   out!? Time for talking is long gone.
16 TYLER: I don't know, man ... Ethan?
17 ETHAN: James, come on ... is this really our fight?
18 JAMES: I do not believe I am hearing this from you two.
19   We've always said we'd back each other up. We'd be
20   there for each other. Was that just talk?
21 ETHAN: No, but ...
22 JAMES: There are no buts. You're either committed to a
23   friendship or you're not.
24 TYLER: I'm his friend, but I don't see a reason to put myself
25   in harms way for nothing.
26 JAMES: If we let those guys get away with beating up Shane,
27   who's to say that they won't come after one of us next?
28 TYLER: Who's to say they will?
29 JAMES: Is that a risk you are willing to take?
30 ETHAN: Is violence really an answer?
31 JAMES: Sometimes, yes, it's the most effective answer.
32 ETHAN: What about turning the other cheek?
33 JAMES: I'm all for that. Twice. That's why God gave us two
34   cheeks ...
35 TYLER: Well, really four ...

1   JAMES: Tyler, shut up!

2   TYLER: I'm just saying ...

3   JAMES: Shut up! And, Ethan, if you're going to start quoting

4   the Bible, let's look at what Jesus did in the temple. I

5   believe he destroyed it ...

6   ETHAN: We're not exactly Jesus, James.

7   JAMES: Oh my God ... do you not see what we have to do?

8   TYLER: Listen, I hang out with those three guys

9   sometimes. I don't need them mad at me.

10 JAMES: What? You hang out with those losers? When?

11 TYLER: When you guys aren't around. I mean, they're not

12   like friends, but we go to the same parties and stuff. I

13   don't need to alienate them.

14 JAMES: So, you'd alienate me?

15 ETHAN: Come on, James. Don't get all testosterone driven ...

16 JAMES: I'm not!

17 TYLER: You kind of are. You're like a bull in a china shop.

18   You want to go in and pound on people without

19   thinking it through.

20 JAMES: You've got to be kidding. Those guys are always

21   beating people up. Today it was Shane. Last week they

22   were pushing Sean around. Remember over the

23   summer when they beat up those kids from Valley

24   High School? Those kids were two years younger.

25   They've been doing this kind of stuff since we were in

26   sixth grade together. It's time to end it.

27 ETHAN: Maybe we should talk to the principal ...

28 TYLER: Or Shane's parents should...

29 JAMES: What good would that do? So they get suspended.

30   Big deal. They get a "severe talking to" by Mr. Roney.

31   Ooooh, that'll shake them up. They've been "talked to"

32   so many times it's ridiculous. You know it as well as I

33   do.

34 TYLER: I still say it's not our place to get involved.

35 JAMES: Tyler, I don't even know who you are. I thought you

1   were a true friend, but it's pretty clear all you have at

2   heart is your own worthless hide. You're afraid of

3   getting hurt, so you let others go down. I'm telling you,

4   you could be next.

5   TYLER: And I'm telling you that, while Shane is my friend,

6   I'm not going to get into a fight because he can't take

7   care of himself.

8   JAMES: Whatever, man. Ethan?

9   ETHAN: Maybe we should talk to them?

10   JAMES: I've talked to them before. You have. They've been

11   suspended a dozen times for intimidation. They're just

12   smart enough to wait until after school to get physical

13   with someone. The time for talk is over.

14   ETHAN: I don't know, buddy.

15   JAMES: Well, I do.

16   TYLER: You're going alone, then. I'm not fighting because

17   someone else can't take care of himself.

18   JAMES: That's fine. Remember those words when three

19   guys come after you. Ethan, you coming?

20   ETHAN: You're sure you want to do this?

21   JAMES: Right is right.

22   ETHAN: I don't know ...

23   TYLER: Ethan, don't be stupid.

24   JAMES: Tyler, don't be a wimp.

25   TYLER: I'm not being a wimp. I'm being smart. This isn't

26   our fight.

27   JAMES: I'm making it my fight. Ethan, Tyler has made up

28   his mind. What about you?

29   ETHAN: Yeah, OK. I'm not going to let you do this by

30   yourself.

31   JAMES: Thanks, buddy. Let's go.

32   TYLER: I hope you don't regret this.

33   JAMES: I hope you don't either. We both have to live with

34   our decisions. At least I know I'll be able to sleep

35   tonight. I hope you can say the same.

1 TYLER: I can. *(JAMES exits.)* Ethan, I hope you're not
2   making a mistake by going with him.
3 ETHAN: We'll see. I'll talk to you later. *(ETHAN exits, TYLER*
4   *is left alone on stage.)*

What Was She Thinking?

Cast: Phil, Greg, Ian
Setting: Inside Phil's house
Prop: Notepad

1 PHIL: Greg, this is going to be such a great night, don't you
2   think?
3 GREG: Oh yeah. Excellent music, and I'm very interested in
4   this Susan girl.
5 PHIL: She's cool. What do you think of Alison?
6 GREG: She's nice. Very pretty. I think the girls will be very
7   impressed at this first date thing.
8 PHIL: Yeah, I think so. They're friends, we're friends, it's all
9   good. Except for one thing. *(He looks at his watch.)*
10   Where's Ian?
11 GREG: Who knows. He said he'd be here at five o'clock.
12 PHIL: Well, it's five fifteen right now. He better show up. I
13   spent hours planning this triple date for us, and he
14   better not screw it up. He still owes me the money for
15   the tickets.
16 GREG: When are you going to learn? You've got to stop
17   fronting him money. He never pays you back.
18 PHIL: *(Pulling a small notepad from his pocket)* Oh, he will.
19   I'm keeping a record.
20 GREG: Did he even get a date?
21 PHIL: He said he would. You never know with that guy. I
22   mean, how hard is it to get a date for a rocking concert?
23 GREG: Tell me about it.
24 PHIL: He's got ten more minutes then we are leaving. And
25   he's still going to pay me the money.
26 GREG: Good luck getting it.
27 PHIL: Oh, don't you worry about that. I'll just pound him
28   and then empty his little Bart Simpson bank he has on

1   his desk and take it.
2 GREG: *(IAN enters.)* It's about time. Phil was going to leave.
3 IAN: Great. *(He flops down.)* It could only have improved the
4   night.
5 PHIL: What's your problem?
6 IAN: My date. If you want to call it that.
7 GREG: You got a date didn't you? Please don't tell me you're
8   bringing your cousin Brett instead.
9 PHIL: You better have a girl, buddy!
10 GREG: Susan won't feel comfortable if you brought a guy ...
11 PHIL: Especially your cousin Brett ...
12 GREG: The guy's a pig ...
13 PHIL: He actually hit on my aunt! My aunt.
14 GREG: She *is* hot ...
15 PHIL: But she's my *aunt!!!*
16 IAN: I brought someone, don't worry. She's a girl ... and I
17   use the term loosely.
18 GREG: I thought you said you'd have no problem getting,
19   and I quote, "any hot little babe," you wanted.
20 IAN: And apparently I was wrong.
21 PHIL: So ... ? Is she at least attractive?
22 IAN: She looks like a biological experiment gone horribly
23   wrong.
24 GREG: Come on, she can't be that bad.
25 IAN: Really? She's waiting outside, take a look.
26 PHIL: *(Looking out the window)* I don't see anyone ... oh!
27 IAN: Exactly ...
28 GREG: Who? The only person out there is ... *(He looks at IAN*
29   *who confirms his guess.)* Ewww.
30 PHIL: Nice hair ...
31 IAN: She seems to think that shaving her head is a good
32   look on her ...
33 GREG: She'd be wrong ...
34 IAN: You think?
35 PHIL: What's with the black around her eyes?

1   IAN: She thinks it makes her look deep and moody ...
2   GREG: If you're a deep and moody raccoon ...
3   PHIL: Who smokes. The girl smokes.
4   IAN: Yeah, she seems to think that smoking says
5   philosophical.
6   PHIL: The hacking cough is lovely ... Hey! Hey! She's
7   grinding out her cigarettes in my mom's flower bed.
8   Hey!
9   IAN: Don't bother. She's got her little earphones in. She's
10   listening to some new band no one has ever heard of.
11   The primary instrument appears to be a jackhammer.
12 GREG: Where'd you dig this girl up?
13 IAN: Look closely.
14 PHIL: I'm afraid she'll hurt my eyes. She's a nightmare.
15 IAN: Yeah ... I know.
16 GREG: Why are you taking her? Was every other girl in
17   school busy tonight?
18 IAN: Look at her. *(GREG and PHIL both look and just shake*
19   *their heads.)* No, really look at her.
20 GREG: What? *(He looks.)* Wait a minute ... can it be?
21 PHIL: What? *(He looks, too.)* Do you know her?
22 GREG: We both know her.
23 PHIL: Greg, trust me. I'd remember that.
24 IAN: Phil, it's Charlene.
25 PHIL: Charlene? Charlene who? *(He really peers out now.)*
26   Charlene?!
27 GREG: What did she do to herself?
28 IAN: Apparently she's had an epiphany.
29 GREG: Since yesterday?
30 IAN: Yeah. Our little blonde homecoming queen has been
31   watching a little too much Oprah. According to her,
32   some doctor was on talking about how everyone needs
33   to experiment, to find their inner poet and explore it,
34   experience it and let it overtake you. I didn't realize
35   that the hot chick I asked to this concert would be

1   inhabited by Sylvia Plath.
2   PHIL: Who?
3   GREG: Suicidal poet. Wrote *The Bell Jar*. Killed herself at
4   age thirty.
5   PHIL: And you know about her because ...
6   GREG: Because I'm in honors English while you wallow
7   around in general ed.
8   PHIL: Ah ...
9   IAN: Most teen girls filled with angst use Ms. Plath as their
10   patron saint.
11   GREG: So Charlene decided that this is a look she wants to
12   go with?
13   IAN: Looks to be.
14   PHIL: And she's going to a worship concert looking like
15   that?
16   IAN: Uh huh. God, she says, is all accepting.
17   GREG: All righty then.
18   *(They all three stare out the window for a moment.)*
19   PHIL: She has a nice shaped head ...
20   IAN: Which is clear to see due to the fact that it is
21   completely hairless.
22   PHIL: Point made.
23   GREG: Come on, Ian. Underneath all that ear piercing,
24   black eye makeup and ... is that a safety pin in her
25   eyebrow?
26   IAN: Yes, sir, you are correct.
27   GREG: Ah. Well, she's still Charlene.
28   IAN: So, you're saying if I blind myself, all will be well.
29   PHIL: It's one answer.
30   GREG: Hair grows back, makeup washes off, piercings
31   close. Now, go out there and be nice. Phil and I will be
32   out in a minute.
33   PHIL: Tell her she can't smoke around me. I'm allergic.
34   IAN: Yeah ... *(Calling out)* Charlene! Char! Char!! *(Making*
35   *movements to match his comments)* Take the earphones

1   out of your ears. Take the ear ... Char! Oh good Lord. *(To*

2   *GREG and PHIL)* **I'll see you out there. Char!!!** *(He exits.)*

3   PHIL: This is going to be an interesting night.

4   GREG: Oh, yeah.

5   PHIL: What do you think Susan and Alison will think?

6   GREG: I don't know. But the way they react will tell us

7   something about their character.

8   PHIL: So, what do we do? Ignore how Charlene looks or say

9   something?

10 GREG: I think we have to say something. I mean, yesterday

11   she had long blonde hair and wore hot clothes. Today

12   she looks like something out of a Winona Ryder,

13   Angelina Jolie movie.

14 PHIL: *(They both look out the window again.)* **What was she**

15   **thinking?**

16 GREG: *(Shaking his head)* **God only knows.**

Five-Minute One-Acts

At the Party

Cast: Julie, Karen, Dominic

Setting: A party

1 JULIE: Did you see who just walked in the door?
2 KAREN: Who?
3 JULIE: Ilene, Heather and Gina.
4 KAREN: Ilene, Heather and Gina who?
5 JULIE: Those freshmen girls Jennifer was telling us about.
6 KAREN: The ones that Dominic is scamming on?
7 JULIE: None other.
8 KAREN: Dominic, get your slimy little self over here right
9   now.
10 DOMINIC: What's the problem now?
11 JULIE: Did you see who just walked in?
12 DOMINIC: Who? *(He looks around.)* Oh, freshmeat ... I mean
13   freshmen.
14 KAREN: You are too low for words. Why are you doing this?
15 JULIE: You and your little friends are pigs.
16 DOMINIC: Doing what? I have done nothing ...
17 JULIE: Yet. I know you and your little gang of users, abusers
18   and losers.
19 DOMINIC: What? I am innocent. I have done nothing.
20 KAREN: Oh no. Just invited freshmen girls to a senior party.
21   I know what happens to freshmen girls. I was once a
22   freshmen girl, you know.
23 DOMINIC: Karen, you survived. They, too, will survive.
24 JULIE: We survived because we had my sister to warn us
25   about what the senior guys do to the young girls. All
26   you care about is getting what you can from them and

1   then laughing about them behind their backs.

2 KAREN: I've seen you in action before, Nicky, and it isn't

3   pretty.

4 DOMINIC: Hey, they're old enough to make up their own

5   minds. It's not like it's rape or anything.

6 JULIE: It might as well be. They don't know any better. They

7   think that if they get together with you it's their ticket

8   to popularity.

9 KAREN: It's their ticket to being called tramp for the next

10   four years, that's what it is.

11 DOMINIC: Hey, no one is twisting their arms, you know.

12 KAREN: Nick, If I see you lay even one hand on those girls,

13   I swear ...

14 DOMINIC: What, you'll beat me up? Listen, maybe if you or

15   Julie would be a little more cooperative ... if you get my

16   drift.

17 JULIE: We get your drift, you sow, but I know Mr. Find 'em,

18   Feel 'em and Forget 'em.

19 KAREN: You left out one "F."

20 JULIE: I know, Karen. And whenever I think about

21   Dominic, I will leave out that one "F."

22 DOMINIC: I am hurt. Truly hurt.

23 KAREN: Get past it, pig.

24 DOMINIC: I plan on it. And now, if you two ladies will

25   excuse me, I see fresh meat on the horizon, waiting to

26   adore my senior status.

27 JULIE: Dominic, I'm serious. They're just little girls.

28 DOMINIC: So little time, so much to teach them.

29 KAREN: Have you no sense of right or wrong?

30 DOMINIC: Listen, girls. You were freshmen once yourself.

31   You managed to make choices when you were tempted.

32   Although, you must admit, you did not have such

33   splendid temptation as myself placed in front of you.

34   But that is beside the point. These girls are here. I am

35   here. All I have to do is pick one.

1   JULIE: I can't believe you'd really do this.

2   DOMINIC: In a flash. Now, which one is Gina? I told some

3   girl that I thought Gina was cute.

4   JULIE: If you don't know which one she is, why'd you say it?

5   DOMINIC: To get her and her friends to come. It worked,

6   didn't it? Now, which one is she?

7   KAREN: The little one.

8   DOMINIC: Perfect. Watch my dust.

9   JULIE: Dominic ...

10 DOMINIC: Later, my friends, later. *(He leaves.)*

11 JULIE: The guy's a pig.

12 KAREN: And those girls are stupid.

13 JULIE: I've seen enough. I'm too old for these parties

14   anymore.

15 KAREN: We're outta here. *(They exit in disgust.)*

Communication Is the Key

Cast: Tina, Martin, Vicki

Setting: School hallway

1 TINA: Martin, Vicki, did you see Matt today?

2 MARTIN: Uh, no, Tina. Vicki, did you see Matt today?

3 VICKI: Matt? No. Nope, I didn't see him.

4 TINA: What's going on? You both are acting very suspicious.

5   Where is he? Martin, I know you know because he

6   doesn't make a move without telling you about it first.

7 MARTIN: Hey, Tina, it's not my hour to watch him, OK? Last

8   time I looked, Matt was seventeen and fully capable of

9   taking care of all bodily functions on his own

10 TINA: That's what I'm worried about. Him taking care of

11   those bodily functions.

12 VICKI: It's a sad and dying relationship that is lacking

13   trust. And you definitely don't trust him.

14 TINA: Would you trust Martin if he were as ... how shall I

15   put this in polite company ... "friendly," as Matt?

16 VICKI: Good point. The guy's a pig.

17 MARTIN: Hold on just a minute, there, girls. You're talking

18   about my best friend.

19 TINA: Are you going to stand there and deny that he cheats

20   on me?

21 VICKI: *(Looking carefully at MARTIN)* Well, are you? You're

22   his best friend, you know how he is.

23 MARTIN: That is the difference between men and women

24   today. Women gossip while men have learned to mind

25   their own business.

26 TINA: Oh, please. Men are just as bad, but they discuss it

27   amongst themselves. Women just share their

28   knowledge with both sexes.

29 MARTIN: Semantics. You call it "sharing," I call it "gossip."

1   Either way, you're still talking about people when
2   they're not here.
3 VICKI: Are you telling me that you talk about me with your
4   little loser friends?
5 MARTIN: Now, how did you come to that conclusion when
6   we were talking about Matt and Tina and their
7   problems?
8 VICKI: Because you just said that men discuss things
9   between themselves and not with other women. I
10   inferred from that statement that yes, indeed, I am the
11   subject to locker room conversation
12 MARTIN: Wait a minute. We're talking about Matt, not me.
13 TINA: It looks to me like your boyfriend has something to
14   hide, Vicki, doesn't it?
15 VICKI: Just what *are* you hiding, Martin?
16 MARTIN: I'm not hiding anything. All I said was that I
17   didn't know where Matt was, and now I'm on trial for
18   my life. I don't get it.
19 VICKI: You're just like all the rest of the men. Two-faced
20   liars.
21 TINA: You tell him, girl. Don't let him treat you like this.
22   I've taken it long enough from Matt.
23 VICKI: You're right. It's time we stand up for ourselves and
24   demand that we are treated with respect.
25 MARTIN: I do treat you with respect. All I said was that I
26   wasn't Matt's keeper, and now I'm a two-faced, lying
27   cheat? What's going on?
28 TINA: Did you hear that? He said cheat!
29 VICKI: Yes, he did, didn't he? Why'd you say "cheat" Martin?
30   I didn't say it, but you did. Guilty conscience?
31 TINA: Think about it, Vicki. He's Matt's best friend. Matt's
32   not here. I bet he has some little freshmen tramps
33   waiting for them at his house.
34 VICKI: Fine, Martin. Go over there and be with those little
35   tarts. We're through. I've had it.

1   MARTIN: But ... wait ... I ... uh ... You are ...

2   VICKI: I am through, that's it, that's all. I've had it.

3   TINA: Come on, Vick. We'll find us some real men. Not

4   these low-life lying little slime ball cheats.

5   VICKI: Good-bye, Martin. Don't bother calling. *(They exit.)*

6   MARTIN: *(Alone on stage)* What just happened here?

How Do I Look?

Cast: Mark, Kelly

Setting: Kelly's living room

Props: *Cosmopolitan* magazine, phone

1 **MARK:** What are you reading, there, Kelly?

2 **KELLY:** The new *Cosmo*.

3 **MARK:** Ah. Mind if I watch the game?

4 **KELLY:** Go ahead. *(They are absorbed in their own activities,*

5   *exchanging a warm smile.)* **Mark?**

6 **MARK:** Yeah, Kel?

7 **KELLY:** What would you change about me if you could?

8 **MARK:** What?

9 **KELLY:** If you could change one thing about me, about the

10   way I look, what would it be?

11 **MARK:** Let me see that magazine.

12 **KELLY:** What?

13 **MARK:** Is this one of those magazine quizzes?

14 **KELLY:** Maybe ...

15 **MARK:** I'm not answering. This is a no win for me.

16 **KELLY:** So you'd change something?

17 **MARK:** I didn't say that.

18 **KELLY:** You said that you wouldn't answer. That's an

19   answer.

20 **MARK:** I wouldn't change anything.

21 **KELLY:** You have to.

22 **MARK:** No I don't.

23 **KELLY:** I mean, if you had to change *something*, what

24   would it be.

25 **MARK:** You are perfect the way you are.

26 **KELLY:** No, you're not getting it. If you didn't change

27   something, I'd die.

28 **MARK:** This is ridiculous. You're not going to die if I don't

1   change something.

2 **KELLY:** Play the game.

3 **MARK:** Good grief.

4 **KELLY:** You know you'd change something if you could. I

5   mean, I'm not perfect.

6 **MARK:** True.

7 **KELLY:** What does that mean?

8 **MARK:** I'm just agreeing with you. Let me watch the game.

9 **KELLY:** *(Taking the remote)* No. Now look at me. *(He sighs*

10   *heavily and turns to look at her.)* What would you

11   change?

12 **MARK:** I don't know ... your hair, I guess.

13 **KELLY:** My hair?

14 **MARK:** Yeah, sure, I guess.

15 **KELLY:** There, was that so hard?

16 **MARK:** Can I please watch the game now?

17 **KELLY:** Of course, darling. *(He returns to the game, she*

18   *stares at him.)*

19 **MARK:** What? What?

20 **KELLY:** What's wrong with my hair?

21 **MARK:** Nothing is wrong with your hair.

22 **KELLY:** But you said you'd change it. What would you

23   change? The length? The color? What?

24 **MARK:** Nothing.

25 **KELLY:** But you said ...

26 **MARK:** You made me ...

27 **KELLY:** Yeah, but you were awfully quick to choose the hair.

28   You just zeroed right in on the hair. Took one look and

29   announced clearly for all the world to hear, "Your hair

30   is a disaster."

31 **MARK:** I did not say ...

32 **KELLY:** You've always had a preference for redheads. Don't

33   think I don't see your eyes practically pop out of their

34   sockets whenever Faye sashays by, with that long, silky

35   red hair swinging in the sunlight.

1   MARK: I'm not looking at her hair ...

2   KELLY: What?

3   MARK: I mean ...

4   KELLY: What are you looking at then?

5   MARK: I didn't say that I was looking at anything ...

6   KELLY: You want to go out with Faye? Is that what you are

7   saying? My hair repulses you, I have become so

8   disgusting to you that you want to break up? Is that it?

9   Well, I don't need this ...

10 MARK: I didn't say that ...

11 KELLY: I think you should leave.

12 MARK: That's fine. I can watch the game in peace. I'll call

13   you later.

14 KELLY: Don't bother.

15 MARK: Yeah, I will. But what will probably happen is in an

16   hour you will realize what a nut case you are and you

17   will call me. Because you know I love you.

18 KELLY: Yeah, well ...

19 MARK: And I wouldn't change a single thing about you. Not

20   one.

21 KELLY: Sure ...

22 MARK: *(He smiles at her.)* Call me on my cell, Kel ... *(He*

23   *exits.)*

24 KELLY: *(She sits, thinking, then takes out her phone and*

25   *dials.)* Mark? Want to grab some lunch in an hour? I'll

26   pay. Yeah, love you, too.

In the Eye of the Beholder

Cast: Janice, Bill, Rocky (a male dog),
Tiger (a female cat)
Setting: Janice's living room, there are at least
two chairs On-stage
Props: Rocky is wearing a bow

1 JANICE: Oh, Rocky, you are so handsome. Look at you.
2   What a handsome boy. Rocky, come in here. *(Calling*
3   *opposite)* Bill, come in here.
4 ROCKY: *(Entering, Rocky has a big bow around his neck. He*
5   *is very proud of how he looks.)* OK, here I am. I'll just sit
6   over here on the chair. *(He goes to chair.)*
7 JANICE: Rocky, please don't sit on the chair.
8 ROCKY: I just had a bath.
9 JANICE: Bill! Come here.
10 ROCKY: You want I should just stand?
11 JANICE: Come here, you handsome boy. *(She sits on the*
12   *floor and pats a spot next to her.)*
13 ROCKY: *(Goes happily and sits on floor next to JANICE.)* OK.
14   *(Puts his head in her lap.)* I love you.
15 JANICE: I love my handsome, handsome boy. You are the
16   best. You know that, right? Don't you? Who's the best?
17   Who?
18 ROCKY: I believe that would be me.
19 BILL: What do you want?
20 JANICE: Say hi to Rocky.
21 BILL: Hey boy! *(ROCKY looks up and smiles at BILL.)* Come
22   here, big guy.
23 ROCKY: OK. *(He gets up to go to BILL.)* What's up?
24 BILL: What's this?
25 JANICE: What?
26 BILL: What did you do to him?

1 JANICE: What do you mean?
2 BILL: Why would you do this? Rocky, take that bow off right
3   now.
4 JANICE: No! He looks great.
5 TIGER: *(Entering, to ROCKY)* Nice bow.
6 ROCKY: Jealous?
7 TIGER: Jealous? Of you? I don't think so. *(Sits on the chair.)*
8 JANICE: Bill, leave Rocky alone.
9 BILL: He's not going to wear this bow.
10 ROCKY: What's wrong with my bow?
11 TIGER: You look like a girl.
12 ROCKY: This from a girl with a guy's name ... Tiiiiger?
13 TIGER: *(Turns her nose up at ROCKY.)* Phffft.
14 JANICE: Come here Rocky.
15 ROCKY: OK.
16 BILL: Rocky, stay.
17 ROCKY: OK.
18 JANICE: Rocky, now!
19 ROCKY: OK.
20 BILL: Rocky! Sit!
21 ROCKY: OK. *(He sits.)*
22 TIGER: Strap on a backbone, buddy.
23 ROCKY: Shut up!
24 BILL: Now, take this thing off.
25 ROCKY: What? Wait a minute.
26 JANICE: You are so mean!
27 TIGER: You look like an idiot. Big guy like you walking
28   around with a giant yellow bow around your neck. I'd
29   like to see someone try that with me.
30 BILL: I'm not mean. You're making Rocky look foolish.
31 JANICE: He looks handsome. Don't you Rocky?
32 ROCKY: Yes, I do.
33 TIGER: You look ridiculous.
34 ROCKY: This is why you don't have any friends. You're
35   unpleasant.

1 TIGER: Really? The boy likes me. I've been sleeping with
2   him for years.
3 ROCKY: You sleep with him? In his bed?
4 TIGER: Indeed.
5 JANICE: Well, at least let me take a picture of him.
6 BILL: Why, so you can torture him later with it?
7 TIGER: Yeah, take a picture. Make me an eight by ten.
8 ROCKY: Shut up! I hate you.
9 TIGER: Don't care ...
10 ROCKY: I hate you!
11 TIGER: I think I'll just take a nap.
12 BILL: You're not going to make my dog look like a girl!
13 ROCKY: Girl?!
14 JANICE: He doesn't look like a girl. He looks adorable.
15 TIGER: Like a girl.
16 ROCKY: *(To BILL)* This bow makes me look like a girl? A
17   girl? Take it off, take it off, take it off.
18 BILL: Come here, boy. I won't let that mean girl take you to
19   that groomer ever again.
20 ROCKY: Thank you, thank you, thank you, thank you.
21 JANICE: How do you expect him to be clean?
22 BILL: I'll just give him a bath myself. Outside, with the
23   hose.
24 ROCKY: Outside, with the hose?
25 TIGER: It's so much better to be a cat. We just clean
26   ourselves, get pet and fed and get to sit on any chair we
27   want.
28 JANICE: Tiger, come here.
29 TIGER: *(Looks up at JANICE, then puts head back down.)* I
30   don't think so.
31 JANICE: *(Going to TIGER)* Such a good kitty.
32 TIGER: You see what I did there? You see that?
33 ROCKY: Cats are just arrogant.
34 TIGER: And dogs walk around with big bows and have to
35   sleep outside. Who would you rather be?

1   BILL: Come on, buddy. Let's go outside and toss the ball.

2   ROCKY: I'd rather be me. I'm going out to play ball. You're

3   not even allowed to go outside.

4   JANICE: Let me get your brush, Tiger Lily, and we'll watch

5   TV and I'll brush you.

6   TIGER: Yeah, go outside and chase after a ball or lay in here

7   and get brushed. You make the call.

8   BILL: Dinner later?

9   JANICE: Sure. Let me know.

10 BILL: Come on, Rocky boy. Lets go.

11 ROCKY: *(Happily and excited)* OK, OK, OK, OK. *(Snarls as he*

12   *passes by TIGER.)* Stupid.

13 TIGER: *(Hissing)* Suck up.

14 BILL: Look at them.

15 JANICE: It's almost like they could talk.

My Dinner with Daddy

Cast: Micah, Bonny
Setting: Inside Micah's house
Props: A thermos of soup, crackers, juice

1 MICAH: Did you bring the soup?
2 BONNY: Yes. And the crackers. Are you sure you can hold
3   down crackers?
4 MICAH: I've got a cold, not the flu. You starve the flu. A
5   cold, you feed. A cold demands food.
6 BONNY: I remember it as starve a cold, feed a flu.
7   Alliteration.
8 MICAH: Yeah, well, you try feeding a flu, my friend, and you
9   will be retching regularly while wasting away. Now,
10   that's alliteration. *(He sneezes.)* Oh, God, let me die
11   now.
12 BONNY: None of that! You have to get well. My father is
13   expecting you at dinner tomorrow.
14 MICAH: I don't see it happening. *(He coughs pathetically.)* I
15   really don't see it.
16 BONNY: Well, mister man, it better happen. Here, let me get
17   you some juice.
18 MICAH: No juice. Seven-up would be good.
19 BONNY: Seven-up is for an upset stomach. Juice is for a
20   cold. What is it you have? Cold or flu?
21 MICAH: Which will get me the Seven-up?
22 BONNY: Don't be such a baby. Have the juice. Seven-up has
23   sugar. Absolutely no nutrional value at all.
24 MICAH: *(Whining)* But I'm siiiick.
25 BONNY: It's my father, isn't it?
26 MICAH: What?
27 BONNY: My father.
28 MICAH: I have no idea what you are talking about.

152

1   BONNY: Every time my father wants you to come to dinner,
2   you manage to get sick.
3   MICAH: Lies! All lies!
4   BONNY: Oh please. What happened last month? Daddy
5   said, "Ask Micah over for dinner for Saturday." So I did.
6   What happens? Friday you break your ankle.
7   MICAH: It happened at the football game. I couldn't help it.
8   BONNY: You broke it stepping off the bus.
9   MICAH: Where was the bus?
10 BONNY: At the game.
11 MICAH: So, I broke it at the football game.
12 BONNY: You are really reaching. OK, look at when my sister
13   was here from college. Daddy invites you, but, no, you
14   come down with some rash.
15 MICAH: Poison ivy. It itched. I was raw for a week. I bled!
16 BONNY: And who told not to scratch? Me. And did you
17   listen? Oh, no, not Micah.
18 MICAH: Bonny, I am sure your father is a great guy. I am
19   sure that it is only a coincidence that flowers wither
20   and animals run whenever he comes near.
21 BONNY: My daddy is a wonderful caring man.
22 MICAH: To you. Charlie told me about *his* dinner with
23   daddy. *(He shivers at the thought.)*
24 BONNY: OK, my father was a little stern. He likes good table
25   manners.
26 MICAH: So he whacks Charlie with his fork for putting his
27   elbow on the table? Not elbows, but elbow ... singular.
28   You heard what your dear old dad said when he saw me
29   sitting in his chair.
30 BONNY: I should have told you about that chair. He doesn't
31   like anyone sitting in his chair. It's a "thing" for him.
32 MICAH: I really think it isn't a crime punishable by death.
33   *(He makes feverish cold noises.)* I am not well. I think I
34   will be home under blankets for at least a couple days.
35 BONNY: You listen to me, Micah Armstrong. You eat this

1   **soup, you drink this juice and you get well right now.**
2   *(She gathers her things to go.)* **I will see you promptly at**
3   **five thirty tomorrow night. Be a man.** *(She gives him a*
4   *kiss on the forehead.)* **Suck it up!!** *(She turns to leave.)* **I**
5   **love you.**
6   **MICAH:** *(Sniffling, coughing, whining)* **I don't feeeel good.**

One Seventeenth

Cast: Sarah, Brett

Setting: School hallway

1   SARAH: Why are we constantly fighting?

2   BRETT: It's like we are constantly at war.

3   SARAH: Well, sometimes I do feel like killing you.

4   BRETT: You're funny. You should consider stand-up
5   comedy.

6   SARAH: Comedy is only one of my many talents. Patience is
7   one as well.

8   BRETT: Is it?

9   SARAH: Yes. I need patience in order to tolerate you.

10   BRETT: Well, you're not exactly a walk in the park.

11   SARAH: Goodness, you're clever. "A walk in the park." Did
12   you make that up yourself? How do you live with such
13   cleverness?

14   BRETT: Shut up.

15   SARAH: Shut up! Shut up? I am cut deeply by your witty
16   remarks.

17   BRETT: Could you just shut up? I'm begging you.

18   SARAH: Men should beg, always.

19   BRETT: Enough, please.

20   SARAH: He said "please." How sweet.

21   BRETT: Sarah, I'm done now.

22   SARAH: Are you?

23   BRETT: Yes.

24   SARAH: I'm not.

25   BRETT: Well, I am.

26   SARAH: Not the first time.

27   BRETT: OK, Sarah.

28   SARAH: You always seem to want to end things, don't you?

29   BRETT: And you always don't seem to know when things

1   have ended.
2   SARAH: Sometimes it isn't clear.
3   BRETT: That might be because you aren't paying attention.
4   SARAH: Not paying attention? I?
5   BRETT: You. You weren't watching the signs.
6   SARAH: Watching the signs. Interesting. So, I missed
7   "signs"?
8   BRETT: I put up signs.
9   SARAH: Here's a thought. How about simply saying what
10   you mean?
11 BRETT: I didn't want to hurt you.
12 SARAH: Didn't want to hurt me? So, you think that avoiding
13   me, avoiding any kind of confrontation would be best?
14 BRETT: It seemed like a good idea at the time.
15 SARAH: Coward.
16 BRETT: Coward? Because I wanted to avoid your temper?
17   Your innate ability to flip out at the least provocation?
18   Your insane techniques for making a scene out of the
19   smallest moments?
20 SARAH: I most certainly do not!
21 BRETT: You do! All I wanted was to have a little freedom ...
22 SARAH: Translation – See other people ...
23 BRETT: Fine, see other people ...
24 SARAH: Without telling me ...
25 BRETT: OK, without telling you ...
26 SARAH: In some circles that would be called "cheating" ...
27 BRETT: I didn't want to hurt you ...
28 SARAH: Oh, how very considerate ...
29 BRETT: I had your best intentions at heart.
30 SARAH: And you call me funny.
31 BRETT: I knew you wouldn't understand.
32 SARAH: What I don't understand is why I gave you a year of
33   my life. I'm only seventeen. I have given you one
34   seventeenth of my life! I was a fool!
35 BRETT: Do me a favor. Just don't flip out again, OK?

1 SARAH: I won't. And you do me a favor. Stay away from me.
2   I don't want to see you around here.
3 BRETT: Here? You mean at school? We both go here.
4 SARAH: You stay on your end of the school, I will stay on
5   mine.
6 BRETT: But we have the same classes.
7 SARAH: I am over fighting with you. Over. Get it? Just watch
8   your step, buddy. *(She walks away.)*
9 BRETT: Crazy girl.
10 SARAH: And don't mutter under your breath ... loser.

Opposing Opinions

Cast: Colin, Alexa

Setting: Inside Alexa's house

1 COLIN: Alexa, we need to talk.

2 ALEXA: OK. You want to talk here or you want to go out?

3 COLIN: I think we should stay here at your house.

4 ALEXA: I'm really hungry, though. Let's go to Mickey D's,

5   get something to eat and we can talk there.

6 COLIN: I'd prefer we stay here.

7 ALEXA: But Colin, I said I'm hungry.

8 COLIN: *(Getting a little annoyed)* And I said we need to talk.

9 ALEXA: We can't talk and eat? Are we mentally challenged?

10 COLIN: Sit down please.

11 ALEXA: But ...

12 COLIN: I'm asking you to sit down.

13 ALEXA: So, you're saying you don't want to go get food?

14   You're not hungry?

15 COLIN: Yes, I'm hungry ...

16 ALEXA: Then let's go ...

17 COLIN: But I don't want to go out ...

18 ALEXA: So, we'll make sandwiches ...

19 COLIN: Sandwiches ...

20 ALEXA: Or salads ...

21 COLIN: I don't like salad ...

22 ALEXA: That's why I suggested the sandwich ...

23 COLIN: But you want a salad ... ?

24 ALEXA: I just want food ...

25 COLIN: OK ... hey, wait!

26 ALEXA: Now what?

27 COLIN: The whole point of me coming over here was to talk

28   to you.

29 ALEXA: So talk. Jeez, Colin, you never get to the point of

1   anything.
2   COLIN: I've been trying to tell you ...
3   ALEXA: Tell me what?
4   COLIN: That ... well ... you see ...
5   ALEXA: Speak Colin ...
6   COLIN: I think we should break up.
7   ALEXA: Oh.
8   COLIN: *(Relieved it is out, finally)* **Yeah.**
9   ALEXA: *(Looking him up and down, then very matter-of-*
10   *factly)* **No.**
11   COLIN: *(Taken aback)* **What?**
12   ALEXA: **No. We're not breaking up. Now, you want roast**
13   **beef or ham?**
14   COLIN: **What do you mean "we're not breaking up"?**
15   ALEXA: **Exactly what I said. No.** *(She smiles.)* **So, which?**
16   COLIN: **Wait a minute. If I want to break up, we're breaking**
17   **up.**
18   ALEXA: **Clearly we have a difference of opinion.** *(He starts to*
19   *speak, she cuts him off.)* **Now, listen. You're hungry,**
20   **right?** *(He nods, confused.)* **Did you know you were**
21   **hungry when you got here?** *(He thinks and shakes his*
22   *head.)* **So, if I hadn't said something, you'd still be**
23   **hungry, right?** *(He nods slowly, unsure of where this is*
24   *going.)* **This breaking up thing is the same. You** *think*
25   **that's what you want, but it isn't. So, you wait here, I'll**
26   **get food.**
27   COLIN: *(He sits, after a moment, calls out.)* **So, we're not**
28   **breaking up?**
29   ALEXA: *(Off-stage, she pokes her head in.)* **Nope. Mustard or**
30   **mayo?**
31   COLIN: *(Shrugging his shoulders)* **You decide what's best.**
32   ALEXA: **As it should be.** *(She smiles and slowly moves off*
33   *while he sits back wondering what happened to his life.)*

The Sensitive Soul

Cast: Paige, Dave

Setting: School

1 PAIGE: I've got a serious case of the Mondays.

2 DAVE: It's Wednesday.

3 PAIGE: I know. How depressing is that?

4 DAVE: It's just a day.

5 PAIGE: But if it is Wednesday and I've got the Mondays,
6   then the only answer can be that I'm off and everyone
7   else is on.

8 DAVE: And that is different today how?

9 PAIGE: It's not. That's my point. I'm off.

10 DAVE: True.

11 PAIGE: There is no one quite like me.

12 DAVE: Ain't that the truth?

13 PAIGE: Are you attacking me?

14 DAVE: I'm agreeing with you.

15 PAIGE: It feels like an attack.

16 DAVE: It's an agreement. Jeez, you're so sensitive.

17 PAIGE: I've the soul of a poet.

18 DAVE: Ah. That's what they're calling it these days.

19 PAIGE: But I am. My heart hurts for the oppressed and the
20   unfortunate. I see the hungry and I ache for them.

21 DAVE: So give them your lunch. You don't need it.

22 PAIGE: I don't *need* it?

23 DAVE: If you're that concerned, give that extra sandwich I
24   know your mom puts in your lunch to some hungry
25   person. You don't need it.

26 PAIGE: Are you saying I'm fat?

27 DAVE: Oh Lord.

28 PAIGE: I *am* fat! I've been working out like a fiend, but I've
29   been sneaking Krispy Kremes on the weekends. My

1   hips are huge, aren't they?

2 DAVE: You look fine.

3 PAIGE: Why do you hurt me so?

4 DAVE: Oh, my goodness.

5 PAIGE: You have no understanding of who I really am. No

6   one does.

7 DAVE: Did you do your math homework?

8 PAIGE: Are you listening to me at all?

9 DAVE: You've got the Mondays, you're sensitive, you feel fat,

10   blah, blah, blah, blah. Get over yourself.

11 PAIGE: You're a cruel man, David.

12 DAVE: Did you do your math? I couldn't figure out number

13   eight.

14 PAIGE: I'm misunderstood by everyone. I will never find

15   my soul mate.

16 DAVE: OK, that makes no sense at all, but I'll let it ride.

17   Number eight?

18 PAIGE: $P_2O_5 = 44\% \ P$

19 DAVE: Hmmm, really? I didn't get that, but I'll take your

20   answer.

21 PAIGE: How can I ever find someone who will be as one

22   with me, mentally, emotionally, physically if everyone

23   else is on Wednesday and I'm on Monday?

24 DAVE: Catch up with the rest of us. What about K?

25 PAIGE: $K_2O = 83\% \ K$

26 DAVE: I really need to pay more attention in class.

27 PAIGE: You need to listen to me! I'm tortured.

28 DAVE: You're self absorbed. There's a difference.

29 PAIGE: You have no poetic soul.

30 DAVE: You have a need for serious psychological

31   intervention.

32 PAIGE: Look into my eyes. See my pain.

33 DAVE: *(He looks directly into her eyes.)* You ready for class?

34 PAIGE: You're hopeless.

35 DAVE: Paige, I love you like a sister, but girl, you are such a

1   drama queen.

2 PAIGE: Sensitive. I'm a Monday person in a Wednesday

3   world.

4 DAVE: Blah, blah, blah, blah.

5 PAIGE: Dave ...

6 DAVE: Look on the bright side. For you it's Monday. But it's

7   really Wednesday, so in your world the school week is

8   only three days and the weekend's closer, because

9   Friday's the day after tomorrow.

10 PAIGE: *(Slightly confused)* OK.

11 DAVE: Class?

12 PAIGE: Class. But I want to talk about this later. *(She exits*

13   *ahead of him.)*

14 DAVE: *(Muttering unhappily under his breath)* Terrific.

15   Can't wait.

16 PAIGE: What?

17 DAVE: *(Covering with a wan smile)* Terrific. Can't wait. *(He*

18   *drags off behind her.)*

Sorry

Cast: Nick, Patty

Setting: Nick's house

1 NICK: *(Visibly angry, and growing angrier)* **Just** leave it
2   alone, Patty. I told you, just drop it.

3 PATTY: Why? Just because you say so? I don't know why you
4   think you're the one who tells me what to do. You're
5   not. I don't have to put up with this ordering around.

6 NICK: Patty, I am really serious. You've been on my case all
7   night about this and I am getting tired of it.

8 PATTY: Well, that's too bad, because I'm not done talking
9   about it. I don't like how you are when your friends are
10   around. You go into this big macho attitude and it's
11   ridiculous.

12 NICK: I told you that I was sorry. Now drop it.

13 PATTY: Well, sometimes sorry doesn't cut it. Sometimes
14   sorry just isn't enough to make up for treating me like
15   a servant in front of your friends. I am a person, too,
16   you know.

17 NICK: I said I was sorry. What do you want from me, blood?

18 PATTY: I want you to act like a normal human being. You
19   don't see Rick treating Cara that way, do you?

20 NICK: As I told you before, Rick and I are two different
21   people. Maybe you should find someone like Rick and
22   just leave me alone.

23 PATTY: Maybe I should. Maybe I should start looking
24   around for something better.

25 NICK: Do it, Patty, go on. Just try. But I tell you here and
26   now, you'll never be rid of me.

27 PATTY: That sounds more like a threat than a promise of
28   love.

29 NICK: You take it any way you want. Just know that it is true.

1   PATTY: Well, let's just see how true it is. I've had enough of
2   this kind of treatment. I don't want to see you anymore.
3   *(She begins to leave.)*
4   NICK: Stay where you are, Patty.
5   PATTY: Make me, Nick.
6   NICK: *(Grabbing her, slamming her in her chair)* I said don't
7   go.
8   PATTY: *(Visibly scared and shocked)* What are you doing?
9   NICK: I said you'd never get rid of me. I mean it. Do you
10   believe me? Do you?
11 PATTY: *(Quietly)* Yes, Nick, I believe you.
12 NICK: Then learn from this. Just shut up when I tell you to,
13   and don't threaten me with leaving. Because the only
14   way you'll leave me is if I kill you. Do you understand?
15 PATTY: Yes, Nick.
16 NICK: Now, just stay there. Don't talk. Just sit there and
17   keep your mouth shut.
18 PATTY: *(After a moment, very scared and quiet)* Yes, Nick.
19 NICK: I'm sorry I had to do this.
20 PATTY: OK, Nick ... OK. *(They both just sit.)*

The Spaz

Cast: Alisa, Brett

Setting: The school library

Props: Notebooks, textbooks, other school supplies, crutches

1   *(ALISA is sitting by herself at a table, looking over some*
2   *notes. Her crutches are under the table. BRETT enters.)*
3   **BRETT: Hey ...**
4   **ALISA: Hey ...**
5   **BRETT: I'm Brett.**
6   **ALISA: Alisa.**
7   **BRETT: OK, then I am in the right place. I'm supposed to**
8   **partner up with Alisa and Sheila. And, since your name**
9   **is Alisa, not a common name, then I guess we are**
10   **waiting on Sheila.**
11 **ALISA: Excellent powers of deduction!**
12 **BRETT: Something I pride myself on.** *(He smiles at her, she*
13   *smiles back.)* **So ... you new around here?**
14 **ALISA: Interesting line. Not exactly fresh, but reliable.**
15 **BRETT: No ... no! I didn't mean to ... I mean ... I ... this is**
16   **embarrassing.**
17 **ALISA: I'm kidding.** *(She smiles again.)* **I am new around**
18   **here, as a matter of fact.**
19 **BRETT: So am I. That's why I was asking. I mean, I wasn't**
20   **hitting on you or anything ...**
21 **ALISA: Oh?**
22 **BRETT: Not that I wouldn't want to hit on you ...**
23 **ALISA: I see ...**
24 **BRETT: I mean ... Good Lord! OK ... can we start over?**
25 **ALISA: Sure.** *(She holds out her hand.)* **I'm Alisa.**
26 **BRETT: Brett. Nice to meet you. So, I guess we're waiting on**
27   **Sheila. Do you know who she is?**
28 **ALISA: No. I'm new to this school.**

1   BRETT: Me, too. Maybe that's why the teacher put us
2   together. Get the new kids grouped up and let them
3   fend for themselves. So ... what do you think about this
4   school?
5   ALISA: It seems OK. Different.
6   BRETT: No kidding. Apparently, it is something they call
7   "full inclusion." And you know what that means ...
8   ALISA: That they include everyone?
9   BRETT: Yeah ... including freaks.
10 ALISA: Freaks? What do you mean?
11 BRETT: *(Leaning in, sotto voce)* Retards, spazes ... you know,
12   freaks.
13 ALISA: Retards and spazes? Really? I haven't seen any, have
14   you?
15 BRETT: Not yet. So far, so good. Have you?
16 ALISA: Not that I know of.
17 BRETT: The teacher told me that one of the girls I was
18   going to work with would be "full inclusion." That
19   must mean Sheila ... which of course means we have to
20   do her work and "make allowances."
21 ALISA: What do you think she will be like?
22 BRETT: All weirded out. *(He does the standard spaz, freak*
23   *movements.)* Duh ... duh ... duh ... look at me, I'm a
24   freak.
25 ALISA: You think she'll be like that?
26 BRETT: Or worse. You never know with those kind. Talking
27   all weird and walking all weird and generally getting in
28   the way of normal people like us.
29 ALISA: Yeah. Darn those freaks.
30 BRETT: They give me the creeps, you know. I told Mrs.
31   Daeley, but she told me that because this is a full
32   inclusion school that I better get used to it.
33 ALISA: Have you ever actually talked to one?
34 BRETT: I guess I will be pretty soon. That Sheila girl is
35   probably clomping over here, taking our study time up.

1   And of course, because she's the way she is, we will
2   have to do extra work. Maybe, if you want, the two of us
3   can get together later and go over the notes for this
4   project? You know, without Sheila the Spaz?
5 ALISA: You want to get together with me? Alone?
6 BRETT: If that's OK. I mean, no pressure. But, you're very
7   nice and pretty, and I would consider myself lucky if
8   you would go out with me.
9 ALISA: That's the sweetest way anyone has ever asked me
10   out.
11 BRETT: So? Yes? Can I meet you in front of the school at
12   three o'clock, and we can go for a soda or something
13   and really get to know each other?
14 ALISA: *(She begins to gather her things.)* Sure, if you don't
15   mind going out with a spaz.
16 BRETT: What?
17 ALISA: Can you reach under the table and hand me my
18   crutches, please? You see, I have to use them to clomp
19   from class to class.
20 BRETT: Oh, man ... *(Mortified, he hands her the crutches as*
21   *she struggles to stand.)*
22 ALISA: And you know what? I'm going to be in front of the
23   school at three o'clock. I guess we'll find out what kind
24   of person you really are. I'm going to "clomp on out of
25   here" and find Sheila, OK?
26 BRETT: Oh, man ...
27 ALISA: Hey, you thought I was nice and pretty two minutes
28   ago. That hasn't changed. So, see you after school. *(She*
29   *smiles, pats him on the back and exits.)*
30 BRETT: Oh man ... could I be a bigger retard? *(Catches*
31   *himself.)* Oops, I better watch that!

The Swan Boat

Cast: Adam, Megan, Brian, Jenny
Setting: A park, in the evening

1 ADAM: That was cool, huh guys?
2 MEGAN: Oh yeah, awesome.
3 ADAM: I love the swan boats. So romantic.
4 MEGAN: The best. Anything with you is the best, though,
5   Adam.
6 ADAM: You're the best, Megan.
7 MEGAN: No, it's you.
8 ADAM: Honey, it's you.
9 MEGAN: Sweetie pie, you're the best. The very best.
10 ADAM: No, baby, you're the pinnacle of the best.
11 MEGAN: You're the zenith ...
12 ADAM: You're the ...
13 BRIAN: *(Cutting them off)* OK, OK, you're both the best.
14   There is no one better. Blah, blah, blah.
15 JENNY: Now enough. Good grief.
16 MEGAN: You two are both in great moods.
17 JENNY: Whatever.
18 BRIAN: Yeah, well ...
19 ADAM: The Swan Ride always puts me in a good mood.
20 MEGAN: Oh, yes it does.
21 JENNY: I don't want to know.
22 ADAM: The romantic lighting, the music.
23 BRIAN: Please, don't go into it.
24 MEGAN: The slow rocking motion of the swan floating
25   lightly over the water.
26 ADAM: Back and forth, swish, swish, swish ...
27 JENNY: I'm begging you to stop ...
28 MEGAN: Your arms around me ...
29 BRIAN: Have mercy ...

1 ADAM: Your head on my shoulder.

2 JENNY: Why do they hate us?

3 BRIAN: It's some conspiracy.

4 ADAM: I'm just trying to set a mood. The Swan Ride is a
5   mood setter.

6 MEGAN: You two need to go with the flow, like Adam and I
7   are.

8 JENNY: Well, you two have been going out for six months.
9   This is our first date.

10 BRIAN: I hardly know this girl and you put us on the Swan
11   Ride.

12 JENNY: How do you think we felt?

13 BRIAN: Pretty stupid, that's how we felt. Am I right, Jenny?

14 JENNY: Yes, Brian. You're right. We felt very stupid.

15 BRIAN: Sitting behind you in that stupid swan, watching
16   you two make out ...

17 JENNY: How much fun do you think that was for us?

18 BRIAN: It was no fun at all, that's how much fun it was.

19 ADAM: We weren't making out ... we were just kissing.

20 JENNY: Oh, please. I know a mac when I see it.

21 BRIAN: We weren't born yesterday.

22 MEGAN: Adam, I told you this wouldn't work. It was a
23   stupid idea.

24 ADAM: I just want my pal Brian to be as happy with a girl as
25   I am with you. I guess Jenny was just a mistake.

26 MEGAN: Jenny's a mistake? There's nothing wrong with
27   Jenny.

28 ADAM: Hey, if a girl can't get her man going in a Swan Ride,
29   then she's not much of a woman.

30 JENNY: I beg your pardon?

31 MEGAN: Adam, how much of a pig can you be?

32 BRIAN: I didn't say she didn't get me going ...

33 JENNY: I beg your pardon?!?

34 ADAM: Face it, Jenny, you're just not Brian's type.

35 BRIAN: I didn't say that ...

1 JENNY: What?

2 BRIAN: *(Caught)* Nothing. Nothing. I didn't say anything.

3 MEGAN: What did you say, Brian?

4 BRIAN: I didn't say that she wasn't my type. I just said I felt

5   stupid in that Swan Ride. That's all.

6 ADAM: So, she did get you going?

7 MEGAN: Adam!! Shut up!!

8 ADAM: I just asked.

9 MEGAN: Well, don't.

10 ADAM: Honey, calm down. Baby, baby, you know that I love

11   you.

12 MEGAN: Knock it off with the "baby, baby" stuff. I told you

13   I hated that.

14 ADAM: You didn't seem to mind it in the Swan Ride.

15 MEGAN: It was dark, you couldn't see my face. I was not

16   smiling.

17 ADAM: Yeah, you were.

18 MEGAN: No, I wasn't. I hate it. And I hate the stinkin' Swan

19   Ride. And you don't kiss all that great, anyway.

20 JENNY: Maybe you want to have this discussion without us

21   around.

22 ADAM: What do you mean I don't kiss great?

23 BRIAN: I think she means ...

24 JENNY: Brian, no. Don't go there.

25 MEGAN: Jenny, let's go to the bathroom. *(They begin to walk*

26   *off.)*

27 BRIAN: You know what that means, Adam.

28 ADAM: Yeah, I do. Hey!! Megan!! I know why you're going in

29   the bathroom. Don't think I don't!

30 MEGAN: I'm going in to go to the bathroom.

31 ADAM: Ha!! You're going in to talk about me! That's what all

32   you girls do when you congregate in the bathroom. I

33   bet you never even pee. You all just talk. You're a bunch

34   of talkers!

35 BRIAN: Jenny, I'll wait for you over here.

1   JENNY: *(Looking at MEGAN's irritated face)* **We might be a**
2   **while**
3   **BRIAN: I'll wait.**
4   **ADAM: Me, too, Megan. I'll be right here ... waiting.**
5   **MEGAN: Whatever.** *(They are off.)*
6   **ADAM: You know that girls don't ever use the bathroom as**
7   **a bathroom, right? They use it to talk.** *(Under his breath)*
8   **Buncha talkers.**

Too, Two Different

Cast: Chad, Joyce
Setting: Chad's house
Prop: Phone

1   CHAD: Joyce, what do you want to do tonight?

2   JOYCE: Why do I have to decide?

3   CHAD: You don't. I just asked you a question.

4   JOYCE: Why can't you just make a decision?

5   CHAD: I thought I was being considerate.

6   JOYCE: Try being decisive.

7   CHAD: OK, fine. We'll go to The Block, have dinner and see

8   a movie.

9   JOYCE: The Block is too crowded on a Friday night.

10 CHAD: It's not that bad.

11 JOYCE: Too crowded. Crowds bug.

12 CHAD: *(Under his breath)* Everything seems to bug lately.

13 JOYCE: What?

14 CHAD: Nothing. So, no Block?

15 JOYCE: I really don't want to go there.

16 CHAD: But you want to see a movie, right? And eat?

17 JOYCE: Yeah, food and film sounds good.

18 CHAD: What and where?

19 JOYCE: You decide.

20 CHAD: I made one decision, now it's your turn.

21 JOYCE: Fine. That French film is playing at the Harbor and

22   we can get dinner at Pasta Bravo after.

23 CHAD: The French film?

24 JOYCE: You know I've been wanting to see it.

25 CHAD: Yeah. But you speak French. I don't.

26 JOYCE: So read the subtitles.

27 CHAD: If I wanted to read, I'd stay home ...

28 JOYCE: Here we go ...

1   CHAD: And I thought you were on that low carb diet. How is
2   Pasta Bravo going to help with that?
3   JOYCE: Are you saying I'm fat?
4   CHAD: No, but you told me you were going to cut the carbs.
5   That's all Pasta Bravo has is carbs.
6   JOYCE: So, I'm fat.
7   CHAD: No! I thought I was being helpful.
8   JOYCE: By pointing out that I'm fat?
9   CHAD: No ... I ... never mind.
10   JOYCE: I don't want to never mind.
11   CHAD: I don't want to do this.
12   JOYCE: Do what?
13   CHAD: Have another meaningless argument.
14   JOYCE: Nothing is meaningless. Everything has meaning,
15   Chad.
16   CHAD: No, it doesn't. And don't quote your psychology class
17   to me, please.
18   JOYCE: Face it, there is more here than food and film.
19   CHAD: No, there's not. You see, that's the difference
20   between us. For you, it's all about what is the
21   underlying meaning behind every phrase, every look.
22   You dig for significance in the simplest things. For me,
23   quite honestly, it is just about what are we going to eat
24   and what are we going to do.
25   JOYCE: You're right.
26   CHAD: Thank you.
27   JOYCE: We are simply two different people.
28   CHAD: Exactly.
29   JOYCE: And we are too different.
30   CHAD: That's what makes us work, Joyce.
31   JOYCE: No, that's what makes it too much work, Chad. And
32   I am tired of it.
33   CHAD: Tired of what?
34   JOYCE: Of this. *(She gathers her things.)* I think it might be
35   best if we took a very long break from each other. I'll

1   **call you.**

2   **CHAD: You're leaving?**

3   **JOYCE: Yes. Face it, I'm a French film ... you're a subtitle.**

4   *(She exits.)*

5   **CHAD: I'm a subtitle? What the heck does that mean?** *(Picks*

6   *up the phone and dials.)* **Kyle? Yeah, it's me. I think Joyce**

7   **just broke up with me ... again. Bothered? Let me think**

8   **about it.** *(Thinking the briefest moment)* **Uh ... no. Not at**

9   **all. Let's head to The Block and catch the new movie**

10   **with The Rock and grab something to eat. I'm starving.**

What Do You Want to Do?

Cast: Paul, Mary

Setting: Mary's house

1   PAUL: Mary, what do you want to do tonight?

2   MARY: I don't know. What do you want to do?

3   PAUL: There's a good movie playing. We could do that.

4   MARY: What's the movie?

5   PAUL: *Rip Tide*.

6   MARY: Paul, all that violence? I don't think so.

7   PAUL: Oh. Well, how about that new Italian movie,

8   *Laughing and Crying*?

9   MARY: Nah. You really want to spend the evening reading

10   subtitles?

11 PAUL: OK. Oh, hey, that new documentary on preserving

12   the wildlife is playing at the Mesa Art House.

13 MARY: Oh, yeah, like either of us really care.

14 PAUL: Instead of a movie, how about a play?:

15 MARY: Like what?

16 PAUL: The touring company of *Cats* is still in town.

17 MARY: Yeah, at sixty-five dollars a ticket.

18 PAUL: Forget that.

19 MARY: We could go to the game.

20 PAUL: Nah. If I'm not playing, I'm just not interested.

21 MARY: Bowling?

22 PAUL: Hurts my thumb. How about going to the beach? We

23   could sit and watch the sunset, maybe make a

24   campfire.

25 MARY: Last time we did that you burned off your eyelashes.

26 PAUL: They grew back in nicely, though, don't you think?

27 MARY: Uh-huh. Hey, why don't we go to Disneyland?

28 PAUL: Again?

29 MARY: It's not like it costs anything. We both have

1   passports.

2   PAUL: I'm sick of Disneyland.

3   MARY: Yeah, me too, really. Knotts?

4   PAUL: Too crowded.

5   MARY: Magic Mountain?

6   PAUL: Too far. Camelot?

7   MARY: I hate miniature golf.

8   PAUL: The mall?

9   MARY: Too many people we know go there. Hey, we haven't
10   gone to the mountains in a long time. That might be
11   fun.

12 PAUL: Those windy roads make me carsick.

13 MARY: You want to go dancing?

14 PAUL: Dancing? No, I don't think so.

15 MARY: Well, I guess we can just sit here all night trying to
16   figure out something to do. At least we will be occupied
17   with some task, no matter how trivial and inane.

18 PAUL: Your parents are gone for the evening. We could just
19   stay in, you know.

20 MARY: Yeah, we could.

21 PAUL: I'm sure we could think of *something* to do.

22 MARY: If we put our heads together, I bet we could think of
23   *something*. *(She smiles.)* You want to eat dinner?

24 PAUL: Now or later? Chinese or Italian?

25 MARY: Oh, great, more decisions. Forget it, we'll eat what's
26   in the fridge and mac on the couch.

27 PAUL: I like a take-charge woman!

Ten-Minute One-Acts

Bittersweet

Cast: Sharon, Carrie, Chris (male)
Setting: Wedding reception

1   SHARON: I don't feel well. I don't feel well at all. Is the
2   room spinning? It seems to me to be spinning around
3   and around. Did you see Hitchcock's *Vertigo*? Around
4   and around and around.
5   CHRIS: Just lie still and you'll be all right in a minute.
6   SHARON: Isn't it interesting how the room can spin into
7   this kaleidoscope of colors and designs?
8   CHRIS: It's a wondrous thing.
9   SHARON: *(Closing her eyes)* But it can make you really sick
10   if you watch it too long. Ohh, I don't feel good. Where's
11   Carrie? Where is the only other single woman at this
12   crummy wedding?
13   CHRIS: So, Sharon, why did you drink so much?
14   SHARON: Did you see the bartender? He's so cute. Soooo
15   cute. And I think he liked me. He kept giving me free
16   drinks.
17   CHRIS: He's giving everyone free drinks. It's an open bar,
18   remember?
19   SHARON: Ah, but is he asking for everyone's phone
20   number? I think not! So, I stayed by the bar and talked
21   and talked and drank and drank.
22   CHRIS: Why didn't you stop drinking?
23   SHARON: Because he kept making up these exotic drinks
24   in all these pretty colors and naming them after me. He
25   made this pretty blue coconut drink he called Sweet
26   Sharon's Blues, so it would take away the blues, he said.

1   Then he made this one out of Midori that he called
2   Jealousy, you know, 'cause Midori is green? He said that
3   if I left him that he'd feel green with envy if I went off
4   with someone else. He made this other one that was all
5   pink called Pretty in Piña because he said my lips were
6   the pinkest, poutiest, most kissable lips he'd ever seen.
7   Are they, Chris? Are they?
8   CHRIS: Yes, sweetheart, they are. Very kissable. *(He gives*
9   *her a warm friendly kiss.)*
10 SHARON: Thank you. You're really a sweetie pie. *(A deep*
11 *sigh)* You and Carrie never should have broken it off.
12 CHRIS: Well, that came out of nowhere.
13 SHARON: *(Seriously)* Whatever happened, really?
14 CHRIS: I don't know. I tried ... *(A look from SHARON)* It
15 takes two to try.
16 SHARON: But if you really care about each other ...
17 CHRIS: There's caring and then there's something else. You
18 know how Carrie always has that emergency cigarette
19 in her bra? That's what I began to feel like. An
20 emergency cigarette. She wanted me, I wanted her, but
21 we figured we were bad for each other. But, she kept
22 me around, just in case she needed me. After awhile we
23 both outgrew our habit for each other.
24 SHARON: What would've happened if you both had given
25 in, just a little?
26 CHRIS: As my sainted granny used to say, "Woulda, coulda,
27 shoulda don't mean sh—."
28 SHARON: *(Cutting him off)* Your granny was one smart
29 cookie. *(She hugs him.)*
30 CARRIE: *(Entering)* Well, well, well, what have we here? I'm
31 informed that my best friend is passing out in the john
32 and instead I find you two entwined in each other's
33 arms.
34 SHARON: Oh, Carrie, I met the most marvelous man. So
35 intelligent, so creative, so sweet, so perfect.

1 CARRIE: So obviously someone other than Chris, I assume?
2 CHRIS: The bartender.
3 CARRIE: Ah! Bartender. Good personal life choice, Sharon.
4 　　　Go for the big future.
5 SHARON: He's sweet.
6 CARRIE: So are these chocolates, but you keep choosing
7 　　　them instead of something with substance and you'll
8 　　　end up empty. Isn't that right Chris?
9 CHRIS: Just in case that comment about no substance was
10 　　　aimed at me, you can drop dead.
11 CARRIE: And ... you're mad at me because why ... ?
12 CHRIS: You can be so condescending, you know that? Never
13 　　　mind, it's not worth it.
14 CARRIE: That's right, it's not. So, Sharon, how are you
15 　　　feeling?
16 SHARON: A little light. A little tight. Oh, I rhymed. I hate
17 　　　weddings, don't you? Aren't they just awful, especially
18 　　　when they're not yours? Don't you want to get married?
19 CARRIE: It's not a matter of just getting married. It's a
20 　　　matter of marrying the right person.
21 SHARON: Do you think my bartender could be that right
22 　　　person?
23 CARRIE: Could be. What's his name?
24 SHARON: I don't know. I just called him Bartender. Did you
25 　　　see him? Such big brown eyes. Eyes only for me, he
26 　　　said.
27 CARRIE: Did he, now? Well, that's very nice. I'm sure as
28 　　　bartenders go, he's one of the finest.
29 SHARON: Are you trying to be funny?
30 CARRIE: No. I just said that he's a fine bartender.
31 SHARON: But it was the way you said it. Huh, Chris. Didn't
32 　　　she say it funny?
33 CHRIS: Sorry, stopped listening.
34 CARRIE: You like the bartender? Great. Go with him, become
35 　　　one with him. Personally, it means nothing to me.

1   CHRIS: *(He mutters something nasty under his breath.)*
2   CARRIE: I'm sorry. We're you talking to me?
3   CHRIS: No. Just reinforcing an old concept.
4   CARRIE: That's supposed to hurt, right?
5   CHRIS: You can be hurt? Really? I thought you'd have to
6   care to hurt.
7   CARRIE: Give me something to care about and I will.
8   SHARON: Did you really not care about Chris?
9   CARRIE: *(Avoiding CHRIS's inquiring gaze)* Do you really
10   think Amy's wedding is the place to discuss my failed
11   relationships?
12 SHARON: You just won't open up, will you? Ever since I've
13   known you, you've been that way.
14 CARRIE: Well, ever since I've known *you*, Chris has been a
15   flake and Andy's been an ass and you ...
16 SHARON: What?
17 CARRIE: Nothing.
18 SHARON: And me, what? Say what you were going to say.
19 CARRIE: You want to have this conversation, fine. And you
20   are like a moth to the dim flame of the biggest loser in
21   the room wherever we go. We could be in a room full of
22   doctors and lawyers and you would find the one lone
23   career bag boy from the Pic 'n Save. Honestly, Sharon,
24   the bartender!
25 SHARON: Just because he's a bartender doesn't mean he's a
26   loser. This probably isn't his full-time job.
27 CARRIE: Oh, that's right. He's probably picking up some
28   extra cash in between doing heart transplants.
29 SHARON: Why are you like that?
30 CARRIE: Like what?
31 SHARON: Nothing is ever good enough for you. No one is
32   ever good enough.
33 CARRIE: I just see things as they are.
34 SHARON: I think you see things as you think they will turn
35   out to be. And everything you see is a negative. Chris,

1   for one.

2 CARRIE: You don't know anything about it. Chris and I had

3   this conversation a long time ago. We both knew that

4   there was no chance for a future there. At least not the

5   kind of future I'm interested in.

6 CHRIS: Did I suddenly become invisible?

7 SHARON: The doctor or lawyer thing?

8 CARRIE: No, not the doctor or lawyer thing. Stability,

9   something you can count on, knowing something is

10   going to work out with sure certainty.

11 SHARON: You notice you said some *thing*. How about some

12   *one?* Chris is one of the good guys.

13 CHRIS: I am still in the room. I know, because I see myself

14   reflected in the mirror.

15 CARRIE: You think I don't know that? I've known it since I

16   was fifteen years old. But there is never going to be

17   anything else there, not while he is the way he is.

18 SHARON: People are who they are, he's not going to

19   change.

20 CARRIE: And neither am I.

21 SHARON: Then it is your loss.

22 CARRIE: So, what you're saying is because I am the woman

23   and I should have a husband, I should lower my

24   standards to snare a man? Not in this lifetime.

25 CHRIS: Lower your standards?

26 SHARON: Maybe your standards are unrealistic.

27 CARRIE: If anyone is unrealistic it's Chris.

28 SHARON: Chris has dreams and goals that aren't

29   conventional. It's part of who he is. He's a good guy, you

30   just can't accept that fact.

31 CARRIE: I don't get it. Why is it Chris is *the good guy*

32   because he is still chasing after some unobtainable

33   dream and I'm the bad guy because I don't want to

34   follow his path? Can't I have my own dreams? Maybe I

35   am conventional, but that's who I am, and that's what I

1   want. Yeah, Chris is one of the good men, but he's not
2   who I want to spend my life with. Not the way he is now.
3 SHARON: Then, like I said, it's your loss.
4 CARRIE: Maybe it's his loss a little, too. You should give that
5   some thought.
6 CHRIS: Why are you two speaking about me like I'm not in
7   the room?
8 CARRIE: I'm sorry. I didn't bring this subject up. I don't
9   even know why we are talking about it. You're a great
10   guy, I've told you that.
11 CHRIS: Oh, yeah. I'm great for a friend, but don't quite cut
12   it as something more. True?
13 CARRIE: If we are going to be honest, then that about sums
14   it up.
15 SHARON: You haven't gone out with anybody seriously
16   since you two broke up.
17 CARRIE: So?
18 SHARON: Maybe you still care.
19 CHRIS: Do you? Do you still care?
20 CARRIE: Of course I do. But I want more out of my life than
21   you want. We're going in different directions.
22 CHRIS: Here we go. I've heard it all before. I'm an actor, I
23   have no future, I don't work at it. Yada, yada, yada.
24 CARRIE: Maybe if you really concentrated and showed that
25   you wanted it.
26 CHRIS: Maybe if I had someone to believe in me.
27 CARRIE: Maybe if you gave me something to believe in.
28 CHRIS: I work hard at what I'm doing.
29 CARRIE: Oh, really?
30 CHRIS: I audition all the time. I work a lot ... a lot.
31 CARRIE: Work implies getting paid, buddy, not this
32   community and little theater stuff you do.
33 CHRIS: It will turn into something. I'm practicing my craft.
34   And I do get paid, but just not enough to suit you.
35 CARRIE: Practicing your craft. What a stupid phrase.

1 SHARON: He says he's always got a job performing
2   somewhere or another. And he gets some money for it,
3   I'm sure.
4 CARRIE: Street mime is not a job, it's an annoyance.
5 CHRIS: I'm not a street mime, I'm a Performance Artist.
6 CARRIE: What happened to being a working actor?
7 CHRIS: My chance will come.
8 CARRIE: You've had your chances and you've thrown them
9   away. Face facts, it's always been more fun for you to get
10   high than it is for you to show up for an audition you
11   might not get. What's that mantra you always chanted
12   to me whenever we had this discussion? "Don't try,
13   don't fail."
14 CHRIS: That's how it used to be.
15 CARRIE: Is it? Well, how nice for you. *(A beat)* What'd you
16   smoke before you showed up here?
17 CHRIS: Nothing.
18 CARRIE: Liar. I know you. Too many successful people here
19   from our past for you to show up straight.
20 CHRIS: You just can't let anything go, can you?
21 CARRIE: Tell me I'm wrong. Tell me how different things
22   are. I'd love to know. You can't, can you?
23 SHARON: He doesn't have to justify himself to you. None of
24   us do.
25 CARRIE: Hey, I didn't ask for this argument.
26 SHARON: Maybe if you weren't so unreasonable.
27 CARRIE: Oh, I'm unreasonable? Why, because I don't
28   accept lowering my sights? Because I want more?
29   Sorry, but I want someone whose career goals include
30   more than tossing a martini together or performing in
31   yet another experimental production of some bizarre
32   and unknown author in a dark and dingy storefront
33   theater.
34 CHRIS: That theater is getting a name for itself.
35 CARRIE: What? Wanna Be Theater, Inc.?

1   **CHRIS:** You just can't give anything different a chance, can
2   you? No, your attitude has always been, "my way or the
3   highway."
4   **CARRIE:** What do you call your attitude? I didn't hear you
5   offering to compromise way back when.
6   **CHRIS:** There can be no compromises in my career.
7   **CARRIE:** Your whole *career,* if that's what you want to call
8   it, has been a compromise. Sharon, he's perfect for you,
9   one of the biggest losers in the room.
10 **SHARON:** God, you can say the cruelest things.
11 **CARRIE:** Truth can often be seen as cruel. *(She exits,*
12   *slamming the door.)*

Disputes

Cast: Willow, Alan, Cherish

Setting: At night, outside a home where a party is going on.

1   *(WILLOW enters, angry and upset. ALAN is close behind.)*

2   **ALAN: Willow, come back. Come on, you don't want to drive**

3   **home, you're too upset.**

4   **WILLOW: You think I'm going to stay here and be**

5   **humiliated, think again.**

6   **ALAN: Give me the keys.**

7   **WILLOW: No way.**

8   **ALAN: Give me the keys to the car. You are not driving**

9   **home in your condition.**

10 **WILLOW: What condition?**

11 **ALAN: You are emotionally out of control.**

12 **WILLOW: Am I? Am I?!? I wonder why. Get out of my way.**

13 **ALAN: Give me the keys!**

14 **WILLOW: I'll give you something, all right.** *(She goes to slap*

15   *him, which he dodges and then grabs her arm.)* **Let go of**

16   **me! I said let go of me!!!** *(She struggles.)*

17 **ALAN: I will when you calm down. Now stop!**

18 **WILLOW:** *(They struggle for a moment, then she quiets.)* **OK,**

19   **OK. I'm calm. You can let go.**

20 **ALAN: You're sure.**

21 **WILLOW: Yes, I'm sure. I'm fine, really I am. I was being a**

22   **little crazy. Let go of me and I will be fine. Really.**

23 **ALAN: OK.** *(He lets go of her.)*

24 **WILLOW:** *(She immediately lands a punch.)* **Keep away from**

25   **me you two-timing, low-life worm.**

26 **ALAN: What are you talking about?**

27 **WILLOW: You think I didn't see you kissing Tiffany?**

28 **ALAN: That was nothing! Nothing! She was showing me**

29   **this new kissing thing ...**

1 WILLOW: Am I stupid? Do I look like a fool to you? You were
2   kissing Tiffany, you were kissing Gina, and I saw you
3   follow Cherish into Mike's room!
4 ALAN: No! Tiffany was showing me how to blow kiss and I
5   was comparing it to Gina's lipping. It was comparison
6   kissing, that's all.
7 WILLOW: So, explain you and Cherish Fox, you miserable
8   excuse for a male.
9 ALAN: What?! We were just talking.
10 WILLOW: Oh, is that what it's called now? Do you think I'm
11   a fool? Do you think I didn't know that you two have
12   been sneaking around behind my back for weeks?
13 ALAN: Lies. Who told you these lies?
14 WILLOW: Only everybody at school. Not to mention
15   everyone at this party. It's a sad day when I am an
16   object of pity to Chuck Thornton.
17 ALAN: Since when do you listen to idle gossip?
18 WILLOW: Since I've seen it with my own eyes. I saw you two
19   go into Mike's room tonight at the party.
20 ALAN: You have no idea what you're talking about. Cherish
21   and I are friends, we were talking. Can't I have any
22   female friends?
23 WILLOW: You don't kiss friends, you hush puppy, crybaby
24   jerk. I will not be disgraced by you. Get away from me.
25 ALAN: Is that what you want? Fine. Just remember, you're
26   the one who drove me away. This isn't my choice. I'm
27   the wronged one here. You have wounded me deeply.
28 WILLOW: Don't make me hurt you!
29 ALAN: You've already hurt me. Profoundly.
30 WILLOW: Just leave, get out. *(He exits.)* What a pig. *(She*
31   *paces for a moment then sits in misery.)* What a pig.
32 CHERISH: Alan? Are you out ... oh, Willow.
33 WILLOW: *(Without any friendliness)* Hey Cherish.
34 CHERISH: I didn't know you'd be out here.
35 WILLOW: *(Composing herself)* Looking for Alan? He just left.

1   CHERISH: Oh. Well, I was uh ... see ya.
2   WILLOW: If you are having a hard time finding him, look
3   for the biggest crowd of females. He will no doubt be on
4   the fringes of them, testing out one tired, insincere line
5   after another.
6   CHERISH: He wouldn't do that.
7   WILLOW: Hey, some people collect stamps. Alan collects
8   broken hearts. He just added mine.
9   CHERISH: That's not true. You know he loves you.
10 WILLOW: To quote an old song, "When he's not with the
11   one he loves, he loves the one he's with."
12 CHERISH: That's not very nice.
13 WILLOW: Well, neither is he.
14 CHERISH: I think he is.
15 WILLOW: Then, by all means, you're welcome to him.
16 CHERISH: What? Why, we're just friends.
17 WILLOW: Don't insult me with such obvious lies, OK? I saw
18   you two going into the back room.
19 CHERISH: *(Caught)* Oh. Well, it's your fault. It's clear you
20   have no idea how to treat your man. So what's he to do
21   but turn to someone like me?
22 WILLOW: Someone like you?
23 CHERISH: Someone who thinks he's adorable, and sweet,
24   and cuddly and in need of a lot of caring.
25 WILLOW: Sort of like a small mongrel dog. Apt description.
26 CHERISH: I can take care of him way better than you can.
27 WILLOW: You want him, you can have him.
28 CHERISH: I can? He's mine?
29 WILLOW: We just broke up, for the millionth and final
30   time. It's over for good.
31 CHERISH: You're sure you don't want him and he's mine?
32 WILLOW: Yep. You win the big booby prize.
33 CHERISH: Just like that? You don't want to fight for him?
34 WILLOW: I think I've given up just about enough of my
35   dignity for Alan Cuthbert. Enjoy, have fun, godspeed.

1   **CHERISH:** Gee, thanks. *(She goes off excitedly.)*
2   **WILLOW:** *(Exhausted)* **Oh wow.** *(She looks up at the moon.)*
3   **So, Mr. Moon, we're alone again. Are you the only male**
4   **in the world that can be counted on? Even you are in**
5   **the habit of fading away on me every twenty-eight days.**
6   **Can't count on any of you ...**
7   **ALAN:** Willow, what exactly did you tell Cherish?
8   **WILLOW:** Exactly? Word for word?
9   **ALAN:** What did you tell her?
10 **WILLOW:** To be honest, it wasn't a conversation that I will
11   go home and enter in my journal.
12 **ALAN:** She said you said that I'm hers now.
13 **WILLOW:** And that should impact my life in what way?
14 **ALAN:** I couldn't believe it. She came up to me and
15   announced that I belonged to her. She said you gave me
16   to her.
17 **WILLOW:** Yeah. I said that we broke up, we were through,
18   and that she could have you.
19 **ALAN:** Have me? Like I was some personal possession of
20   yours?
21 **WILLOW:** I told her if she wanted you, she could have you.
22   What's the big deal?
23 **ALAN:** So, you gave me away.
24 **WILLOW:** Like a stick of gum at the bottom of my purse.
25 **ALAN:** Just like that?
26 **WILLOW:** Essentially. It's not like you really care, is it?
27 **ALAN:** Why should I care? You obviously don't.
28 **WILLOW:** I think you know I cared. Past tense. It's over, and
29   now Cherish can have her little plaything.
30 **ALAN:** Is that all I am to you, some plaything?
31 **CHERISH:** *(Entering)* **Alan, where'd you go?**
32 **WILLOW:** It's not all you *are,* it's all you *were.*
33 **CHERISH:** Alan! I'm calling you.
34 **ALAN:** I'm out here. I needed some air. *(To Willow)* **We little**
35   **playthings do need to breathe, you know.**

1 CHERISH: Willow said she doesn't want you anymore, and
2   so I get you. Isn't this great? We don't have to sneak
3   around anymore.
4 WILLOW: Aha! So you were sneaking around.
5 ALAN: No, no! We weren't. Cherish, it's sneaking around
6   when I come over your house and we aren't seen in
7   public.
8 CHERISH: But you said that Willow would be mad if ...
9 ALAN: Forget what I said.
10 WILLOW: By all means, forget what Alan says, Cherish.
11   Because his stories switch from one day to the other. I
12   hope you two are very happy together.
13 CHERISH: *(Grabbing his arm)* Alan, you're all mine.
14 ALAN: Am I?
15 CHERISH: Uh-huh. Willow said it was OK, didn't you
16   Willow?
17 WILLOW: You two have my blessing.
18 ALAN: Did it ever occur to either of you that I am a human
19   being? I am not some piece of property to be handed
20   back and forth from one woman to another.
21 WILLOW: What the heck? You've been passing yourself
22   back and forth from one woman to another since you
23   hit puberty. So, this time we cut out the middleman
24   and handed you over.
25 ALAN: Am I not human? Do I not get a choice?
26 CHERISH: A choice? Why do you need a choice? You mean
27   you don't want to be with me?
28 ALAN: I'd like some say in it, you know.
29 CHERISH: So, say.
30 ALAN: I've got nothing to say now. I'm pretty upset.
31 WILLOW: Oh, yeah, I just bet you are.
32 ALAN: I am. You two have a lot of nerve treating me like I'm
33   some sort of belonging, like a favorite purse or pair of
34   shoes.
35 WILLOW: Trust me, I wouldn't be giving up a favorite

1   purse or pair of shoes quite so easily. *(WILLOW and*
2   *CHERISH share a girl giggle.)*
3   ALAN: Laugh all you want, but I'm serious.
4   WILLOW: Oh, are you? Is the big man serious? Have we
5   hurt his wittle bitty feelings?
6   ALAN: I thought you cared about me, about us. And you,
7   Cherish, to take from Willow what she so obviously
8   sees as her discards. What does that say for you?
9   CHERISH: Discards? Like I get what she doesn't want?
10 WILLOW: Well, that's what he is.
11 ALAN: Am I? Are you sure?
12 CHERISH: Wait a minute. Did you two break up or not?
13 ALAN: Did we?
14 WILLOW: I guess. I suppose. I ... well, uh ...
15 ALAN: We always go through these little spats.
16 CHERISH: Is he mine or not?
17 WILLOW: Show the man some respect. He's not a toy.
18 CHERISH: You just said you didn't want him.
19 WILLOW: I don't, but ...
20 CHERISH: Well, if you don't want him, I get him.
21 WILLOW: Over my dead body.
22 CHERISH: That can be arranged.
23 ALAN: *(Obviously enjoying this)* Now girls ...
24 CHERISH: You stay out of this ...
25 WILLOW: Don't talk to him that way.
26 CHERISH: Don't tell me how to talk to anyone. You threw
27   that man away ...
28 WILLOW: Threw him away? You practically ripped him out
29   of my arms.
30 CHERISH: Well, think again. Look at you, some sorry little
31   skinny thing with no idea of how to hang on to any kind
32   of real relationship ...
33 WILLOW: How to hang on? What do you think I've been
34   doing besides hanging on?
35 CHERISH: Learn to love instead of cling!

1　WILLOW: *(Raising her hand in a stop sign fashion)* **Talk to**
2　　　**the hand. Talk to the hand!**
3　ALAN: **Ladies, please. I can't stand here and watch this.** *(He*
4　　　*sits.)*
5　WILLOW: **You stay out of this. This is between me and this**
6　　　**little tramp.**
7　CHERISH: **Come on, Alan, you're mine now. We're leaving.**
8　ALAN: **Is this what you really want, Willow? To see me walk**
9　　　**off with another woman, especially Cherish?**
10　CHERISH: **She said you're through ... What do you mean**
11　　　**"especially Cherish?"**
12　ALAN: **Not a thing. It's just that she's always been a little**
13　　　**jealous of you.**
14　WILLOW: **Jealous of Cherish Fox? I think not.**
15　ALAN: **I remember you saying that she had to have had**
16　　　**some kind of surgery to look that way.**
17　WILLOW: **Well, look at the girl.**
18　CHERISH: **Yeah, look. Pretty good, huh?**
19　WILLOW: **Sweetheart, I've known you since seventh grade.**
20　　　**You don't grow those over one summer without some**
21　　　**sort of surgical expertise to help you along.**
22　ALAN: **You're not going to let her get away with that, are**
23　　　**you?**
24　CHERISH: **I am not! Just because puberty has been unkind**
25　　　**to you is no reason to take it out on others who have**
26　　　**been dealt with much more generously.**
27　WILLOW: **Listen, long and lean lasts a lot longer than short**
28　　　**and full bodied. Take a look at the elephant that passes**
29　　　**for your mother if you need convincing of that,**
30　　　**Cherish. If that's your real name.**
31　CHERISH: **What do you mean, if that's my real name?**
32　WILLOW: **Come on, get real. What parent in their right**
33　　　**mind would name a baby girl Cherish Fox? That name**
34　　　**has a built in destiny.**
35　CHERISH: **A built in destiny? What?**

1   WILLOW: You have no choice but to be a stripper at some
2   tacky little roadhouse on Interstate Five. It's your
3   karma, your kismet, your fate.
4   CHERISH: OK, *Willow*. Get a real name!
5   WILLOW: My name has meaning! Strong, but yielding.
6   CHERISH: I think your mom watched too many soaps
7   while she was pregnant with you. Which would explain
8   your need to over dramatize every situation like some
9   really bad actor. You never let a moment go by without
10   some huge reaction to it. You just have to be the center
11   of everyone's attention, don't you?
12   ALAN: Are you going to let her talk to you that way?
13   WILLOW: I most certainly am not. I ... *(She looks at ALAN.)*
14   CHERISH: I'm ready, come on. Well, what are you waiting
15   for?
16   WILLOW: Alan, you are loving this, aren't you?
17   ALAN: I most certainly am not. I am shocked and appalled
18   by your behavior, both of you. However, if you feel the
19   need to have this ridiculous catfight, far be it from me
20   to interfere.
21   CHERISH: You know something? I think he wants us to
22   fight over him.
23   WILLOW: You're right, he does. Well, my dear boy, perhaps
24   in another dimension, in another place and time.
25   ALAN: You never loved me.
26   WILLOW: Why? Because I won't get into some hair pulling
27   girl fight with Cherish?
28   ALAN: No, not because of that. Because love is trust, love is
29   honesty and caring, love is believing in someone, love
30   is ...
31   WILLOW: Never having to say you're sorry? Excuse me, my
32   friend, but bad movie dialogue is not my style. Listen,
33   your definition of love is far different from mine. I will
34   not be lied to, deceived or made a fool of by you ever
35   again. *(To CHERISH)* Like I said, you want him, you can

1   have him.

2   ALAN: Your loss, babe. Come on, Cherish. You know how to

3   hang on to a man.

4   CHERISH: You really wanted me to fight for you, didn't you?

5   ALAN: Fight is such a strong word. What I wanted was to

6   see who cared the most about me. Who would go that

7   extra mile.

8   CHERISH: Extra mile? You want me to go an extra mile?

9   And what do I get in return for this mileage?

10   ALAN: A man who will cherish you. Just like your name.

11   CHERISH: Uh-huh. And how would you be doing that? The

12   same way you "cherished" Willow? By sneaking around

13   on me?

14   WILLOW: You go, girl.

15   ALAN: It was different with Willow. She didn't understand

16   me the way you do.

17   CHERISH: The way I do? You mean understanding how you

18   play one woman off against another? How you toy with

19   emotions like a cat with a bird? You know what I

20   understand? I understand that you are a jerk.

21   ALAN: So, what are you saying?

22   WILLOW: I think she's saying she doesn't want you after all.

23   CHERISH: That about sums it up.

24   ALAN: Is that what it is? You don't want me? Either of you?

25   *(They look at him blankly.)* Well, fine. There are plenty

26   of others in that party that do. You two can just stay out

27   here alone. *(He begins to exit.)*

28   WILLOW: Alone? Oh, I don't think so. You know something,

29   you are beginning to make even Chuck look pretty

30   darn good.

31   ALAN: *(Stopping)* **That was low.** *(He exits as the girls share an*

32   *ironic laugh, exiting the opposite direction.)*

33

Going to the Top

Cast: A, B (The pronouns "him," "his," "he" are
generic. The actors may be male or female)
Setting: The entire scene takes place in an elevator,
depicted through actor's movements to
indicate small space.
Prop: A fake knife

1   *(A enters the elevator, the door starts to close. B calls out*
2   *to hold it.)*
3 **B: Hey, hang on please.**
4   *(A holds for him. B enters, nods thanks. They stand in*
5   *silence while it moves, looking up at the passing floor*
6   *numbers.)*
7 **A: Going to the top floor?**
8 **B: Sure. Why not?**
9 **A:** *(Reaching for the control)* **Oh, sorry. Did you want a**
10   **different floor?**
11 **B: Nah.**
12 **A: Because I'm going to the top floor.**
13 **B: You look like it.**
14 **A: I beg your pardon?**
15 **B: You know, you look like you're on your way to the top.**
16 **A: Oh. Well ... thanks.**
17 **B: Sure.**
18 **A: Do you work in this building?**
19 **B: Nope.**
20 **A: Customer?**
21 **B: Nah.**
22 **A: Visiting a friend?**
23 **B:** *(Snorting in disdain)* **No.**
24 **A: Oh.**
25 **B:** *(Mumbling)*

1   A: **I'm sorry, what was that?**

2   B: **I'm talking to myself.**

3   A: **Sorry. I thought you were talking to me.**

4   B: **Uh-huh.**

5   A: **Did you want to talk to me?**

6   B: **You're nosy, aren't you?**

7   A: **Sorry. I just thought ...**

8   B: **And apologetic. What is that? The millionth time in the**

9   **past two minutes that you've said "sorry." Nosy, and**

10   **apologetic. That's really annoying.**

11 A: **I'm sorry ...**

12 B: **Sorry ...**

13 A: **I didn't mean ...**

14 B: **Are you always sorry?**

15 A: **I just thought ...**

16 B: **Never mind.**

17 A: **Fine. OK.**

18 B: **Just shut up, OK?** *(A starts to speak.)* **I mean it.**

19   *(They stand in silence for another moment.)*

20 B: **Is this the slowest elevator in the history of modern man,**

21   **or is it just my imagination?** *(A gives B a sideways glance,*

22   *doesn't answer.)* **I'm talking to you.**

23 A: **Oh. I, uh ...**

24 B: **Never mind.** *(A glances at his watch.)* **Nice watch.**

25 A: *(Pulling down his sleeve)* **Uh, thanks. My father gave it to**

26   **me.**

27 B: **Isn't that nice? Daddy gave his boy a watch. Sweet.**

28   *(Looking up)* **Did you hear that?**

29 A: **I didn't hear anything.**

30 B: **Someone is talking. Listen.**

31 A: *(Listening)* **Probably just people on the floors we're**

32   **passing. The elevator's moving so slow the voices can**

33   **seep in.**

34 B: **Seep in.** *(He begins to examine his hands.)* **My hands look**

35   **like they belong to someone else.** *(He continues to*

1   *examine his hands with true interest as A watches out of*
2   *the corner of his eye. B chants to his hands in a sing-song*
3   *manner.)* **Little hands, little hands, to whom do you**
4   **belong? Why do you move in a rhythm like a song?**
5   **A: This is a slow elevator.** *(He pushes the floor panel button.)*
6   **B: I told you.** *(Relishing the words)* **The voices can seep in.**
7   **A: Yeah.** *(Hitting buttons)*
8   **B: Don't ...**
9   **A: OK ...**
10   **B: Do you ever look at your hands and wonder what they**
11   **will do next?**
12   **A: You know, I have some business on the next floor. Maybe**
13   **I'll just get off there.**
14   **B: Like sometimes they just hang there ...**
15   **A: I bet someone wants to get on this thing on the next floor.**
16   **B: Sometimes they just take hold of something and squeeze**
17   **like they have a mind of their own.**
18   **A: Is it hot in here?**
19   **B: Then they just move,** *pow,* **like they have epilepsy or**
20   **something. Like now.** *(His hands start moving as if he*
21   *has a bad case of the shakes. He looks surprised at his*
22   *hands' movements.)*
23   **A: Really? Interesting. Oh, hey, the fortieth floor. I can get**
24   **off there.**
25   **B: I thought you were going to the eightieth floor.**
26   **A: I can walk the rest of the way. Exercise will do me good.**
27   **B: Suit yourself.** *(His hand thrusts forward to the floor panel*
28   *and the elevator stops.)* **Oops.**
29   **A: Oops? What the hell?**
30   **B: Don't swear at me.**
31   **A: What did you do?**
32   **B: And don't raise your voice.**
33   **A: You stopped the elevator.**
34   **B: I didn't. My hands did. I was just standing here.**
35   **A:** *(Shouting)* **Move.**

1 B: I said don't yell at me.

2 A: I'm not yelling. Move, so I can get this thing going.

3 B: What's your hurry?

4 A: No hurry. I just want to get moving.

5 B: That's the problem with people today. No one wants to
6   talk.

7 A: *(Hitting the buttons on the panel)* Great. Just great. I think
8   it's broken.

9 B: *(Sitting on the floor, he holds up his hand.)* See this?

10 A: Maybe this button will work.

11 B: I've got this weird callous here.

12 A: No. Come on ...

13 B: Right here on this finger. My ring finger.

14 A: The phone! There's always an emergency phone on these
15   things.

16 B: I don't know why I call you the ring finger. I don't wear a
17   ring.

18 A: *(He opens the box and finds the phone.)* Yes!

19 B: It doesn't make any sense, really, because I don't use this
20   finger.

21 A: *(Into the phone.)* Hello? Hello?

22 B: Do you see it? Right here.

23 A: I don't believe this. It's dead.

24 B: *(Interested for a moment.)* Dead?

25 A: As a doornail.

26 B: Now, how would I get a callous here? Makes no sense.

27 A: *(Looking at the ceiling.)* Maybe if I moved that panel I
28   could climb up there.

29 B: *(His hands start moving again.)* Uh oh, here they go again.
30   *(He wraps his hands around A's feet.)*

31 A: What the ... ?

32 B: Quiet!

33 A: What are you doing, you little freak?

34 B: I told you, it's not me. It's the hands. The stranger's
35   hands.

1 A: Well, get them off of me before I ...
2 B: I told you ...
3 A: I'm telling you ...
4 B: ... no swearing ...
5 A: ... let me go ...
6 B: ... Stop moving! Stop moving ...
7 A: ... get off! Get off ...
8 B: ... It's not me. I can't ...
9 A: This is the last time ...
10 B: You're hurting me ...
11 A: Let go! ...
12 B: *(He frees himself from A and cowers in a corner.)* **No, no,**
13   **no, no, no, no, no, no ...**
14 A: What's wrong with you?
15 B: Don't hurt me. Don't hurt me. Don't hurt me.
16 A: Oh great. Trapped in an elevator with a psycho.
17 B: *(Whimpering)* **Don't. Don't. Don't. Don't.**
18 A: Don't what? I'm not doing anything.
19 B: The walls ...
20 A: What about the walls?
21 B: The walls.
22 A: You scared?
23 B: *(He just whimpers.)* **Ooooh ooooh ooooh ...**
24 A: Not so tough in tight spaces, are you Mr. Strange hands?
25   A little claustrophobic?
26 B: Maybe ... yeah, I am. Just stay away.
27 A: There's not too many places I can go, seeing how we're
28   trapped here in this really small box together. *(He looks*
29   *up.)* **Uh oh, I think the walls are starting to close in.** *(He*
30   *moves closer to B.)* **Yep. Tighter and tighter.** *(He laughs*
31   *unsympathetically.)* **Inch by inch.**
32 B: *(Looks at his hands. He talks to his hands, while A thinks B*
33   *is talking to him.)* **What happened? Did you do this? You**
34   **shouldn't have done this. It was bad.**
35 A: I didn't do anything. *(He slaps him a bit to shake him up.)*

1   Snap out of it. *(B whimpers more.)* **Pathetic. Look at you.**
2 B: **You shouldn't have done it.**
3 A: **I didn't. You're the one who started hitting all the**
4   **buttons.**
5 B: **Liar!**
6 A: **You hit all the buttons, going nuts on me. You try to act**
7   **like a tough guy. You're nothing. Nothing.**
8 B: **You better stop!**
9 A: **Why? You're shivering on the floor like a little girl who**
10   **peed her pants.**
11 B: **Stop! Stop!**
12 A: **Come on. Stand up.** *(He reaches for B.)*
13 B: **It's happening. Get away. Get away. Get away.**
14 A: *(Grabbing B)* **Knock it off, you little punk. Your kind**
15   **make me sick. You think you're so tough, but get in a**
16   **tight spot and you collapse.**
17 B: **I'm begging you.**
18 A: **I could knock you into next week. It would probably be**
19   **good for you. Your kind are all alike. Big man until you**
20   **have to actually be a man.**
21 B: **No. Don't.**
22 A: **Can't take the truth.** *(He softly slaps B across the face in a*
23   *mocking manner.)* **Come on, let's see what kind of guy**
24   **you are.** *(He pushes B around, intimidating him like a cat*
25   *with a broken bird.)* **You gonna just take this? Big guy?**
26   **Big man?**
27 B: *(His hands over his face)* **Stranger's hands. Stranger's**
28   **hands. Stranger's hands. Stranger's hands.**
29 A: **You make me sick. This isn't even fun to bat you around.**
30 B: **No. Don't.**
31 A: *(Sitting next to B on The floor)* **I said I wasn't, you sorry**
32   **idiot.** *(There is a moment of silence while A stares*
33   *straight ahead and B looks at his hands.)*
34 B: **It's so quiet.**
35 A: **Yep.**

1   **B: The callouses are on the fingers. How does that happen?**

2   **A: Just shut up about the callouses. No one cares.**

3   **B: I know. No one cares. No one cares. No one cares.**

4   **A: Maybe the phone will work. Maybe I didn't do it right.**

5   **B: Callouses and no one cares.**

6   **A:** *(He gets up to try the phone again.)* **Maybe there's a secret**

7   **code.** *(While he is at the phone, B stands behind him, we*

8   *can't see what he is doing.)*

9   **A: Dial three-five-two. OK, I did that.** *(His voice changes, he*

10   *drops to his knees.)* **Dead.**

11   **B:** *(Standing behind him, holding the knife that he pulls out*

12   *of A's back.)* **Dead as a doornail.**

13   **A: What have you done ... ?**

14   **B:** *(Shaking his head, looking at his hands)* **Stranger's hands.**

15   **Stranger's hands. Stranger's hands.** *(The lights fade to*

16   *black.)*

Hostage

Cast: Jack, Stacy

Setting: A deserted area, perhaps a garage. Set is
minimal, only one or two chairs or boxes.

Prop: Fake gun, a sheet of paper with a list on it,
a shovel

1   JACK: *(Being pushed onto the stage)* **You're crazy. You're not**
2   **going to get away with this.**
3   STACY: **Sit down. Don't talk, just sit down.**
4   JACK: **No ...**
5   STACY: **Do you not see the gun in my hand? Are you blind as**
6   **well as stupid? Sit down.**
7   JACK: **Fine. Just calm down. What is going on with you?**
8   STACY: **You don't know? Then you** *are* **a moron.** *Sit down.*
9   JACK: **I'm sitting. Just put the gun away.**
10 STACY: **The only place this gun is going is off, directly into**
11   **your pea brain if you don't do exactly as I say.**
12 JACK: **OK. Fine. I'm sitting. I'm listening.**
13 STACY: **Shut up. Just shut up.**
14 JACK: *(After a moment of silence as STACY paces.)* **Are you**
15   **going to tell me why I'm here or are you going to make**
16   **me guess?**
17 STACY: **For someone with very little going for him in the**
18   **way of luck, you have a big mouth. If I have to tell you**
19   **to shut up one more time, I am going to shut you up by**
20   **shoving this gun down your throat. Now, let me think.**
21   *(She paces.)* **OK.** *(She refers to a list she takes out of her*
22   *pocket.)* **Get gun. Got that. Get gas credit card, got that.**
23   **Get Jack.** *(She smiles a menacing smile in his direction.)*
24   **Oh, I got that. Get shovel. OK, that should be back here**
25   *(She looks, finds it.)* **Good, here it is. Call Heidi, tell her**
26   **everything is set. I'll do that in a minute. Pick up**
27   **cleaning.**

1   JACK: *(He has been listening to this listing.)* **Pick up**
2   **cleaning? Get gun, get shovel, call Heidi, *pick up***
3   ***cleaning*? How do you figure cleaning into the list?**
4   **What's going on?**
5   STACY: **My dry cleaning is ready to be picked up. And what**
6   **business it is of yours I have yet to figure out. I'm the**
7   **one with the gun here. If anyone is going to ask**
8   **questions, it will be me. So, shut up.**
9   JACK: **You are crazy.**
10 STACY: **You want to see crazy?** *(Puts gun barrel in his*
11   *mouth.)* **Who's crazy now, jerk? Huh? Who's crazy now?**
12   **I think it's the big man with the big mouth. You want to**
13   **know why you're here? I'll tell you. You're here to pay.**
14   **And pay big. You're going to do the Jesus Christ thing**
15   **for all *man*kind. You're going to die for the sins of men.**
16   *(She takes gun down.)* **Whaddya have to say now, big**
17   **guy?**
18 JACK: **What do you mean I'm going to die?**
19 STACY: **Isn't that just like a man? I tell you you have to die**
20   **for the *sins of all mankind,* and all you catch is the part**
21   **about you dying. You don't pay any attention to the sins**
22   **of man. So typical, "me, me, me" is all you care about.**
23   **Well, big guy, it's time to pay.**
24 JACK: **OK, OK. Sins of man. What sins. Why me?**
25 STACY: **For every woman who has been held back, held**
26   **down, held over and just plain held by some lying piece**
27   **of garbage like you, you are going to pay the price.**
28 JACK: **I haven't done anything.**
29 STACY: **Oh, haven't you? You make me sick. You're going to**
30   **tell me you don't remember when we were in fifth**
31   **grade when I was standing on the swings and you**
32   **knocked me over? I fell on my face, in front of**
33   **everyone. You remember that?**
34 JACK: *(Laughing a little)* **Yeah, your dress went up over your**
35   **head and your underwear ...** *(He sees STACY's menacing*

1   *look.)* **Hey, it was a joke. I was a kid.**

2   **STACY: Yeah, and so was I. A little girl laying on the ground**

3   **with her dress up over her head and her Monday**

4   **underwear on. And it was Friday, Jack. Friday!!**

5   **Everyone said that I had on the same underwear for a**

6   **week. People called me "Dirty Shorts" for the rest of**

7   **that year. In fact, some people still call me that. People**

8   **that you still hang out with, Jack. Your friends.**

9   **JACK: It was a joke, for crying out loud.**

10 **STACY: Yeah, some joke. I've been laughing for years. Ha.**

11   **Ha. Ha. Really funny.**

12 **JACK: OK, OK. I'm sorry. It was mean. I was wrong. But that**

13   **is no reason to hold me here, with a gun to my head. My**

14   **mom doesn't even know where I am.**

15 **STACY: Oh, she'll know soon enough, sweetheart. She'll**

16   **know.**

17 **JACK: What does that mean?**

18 **STACY: The TV has a way of reporting these things.**

19 **JACK: Things? What things? What are you planning?**

20 **STACY: Planning. Yes, planning. That's what I've been**

21   **doing for a long time. And not just me. A lot of us have**

22   **been planning this day.**

23 **JACK: A lot? Who? Why?**

24 **STACY: I told you. Retribution, penance, payback. And you,**

25   **among all the guys we know have been chosen. You are**

26   **the one we feel most deserving of this honor.**

27 **JACK: Oh, man.**

28 **STACY: That's what I like about you, Jack. You have a way**

29   **with words.**

30 **JACK: OK, wait. Lets just talk this over. Let's all just calm**

31   **down here. We can sort this out together.**

32 **STACY: You want to talk? OK, lets talk. You start ...**

33 **JACK: Good, talking. We'll talk. Everyone just calm down**

34   **and we'll talk.**

35 **STACY: Hey, buddy, I am calm. I've got no reason to be nervous.**

1   But I can see how you would be. After all, you're the one
2   with the forty-five trained on your forehead.
3   JACK: You're right. OK, I'm calm, too. Because I know that
4   this is just some sort of joke. Something to scare me.
5   And it's working. Working real well. 'Cause I'm scared,
6   Stacy. Is that what you wanted? Because if it is, you did
7   your job great. I bet you have other people in here,
8   hiding, watching me sweat. *(Calling out)* OK, everyone,
9   you can come out now. The joke is over. Stacy scared
10   me good. You guys really got me. I guess we're even,
11   huh? Tell 'em Stacy. Tell them the joke is over.
12   STACY: You have no idea how close to right you are. The
13   joke is almost over, Jack, and the joke is you. *(She puts*
14   *the gun next to his temple.)*
15   JACK: Oh, God, no, no, no, no. This isn't funny. This is sick.
16   This is too weird. You're never going to get away with
17   this.
18   STACY: Why not?
19   JACK: Because you won't. People don't get away with
20   murder. This isn't TV.
21   STACY: Man, you are so pathetic. How does it feel to be you
22   right now? To be crawling and sweating?
23   JACK: It feels bad, really bad.
24   STACY: Does it? Get out of the chair, Jack. *(He sits and looks*
25   *at her blankly.)* I said get out of the chair. *Don't make me*
26   *get crazy!* *(He quickly rises, she still holds the gun on*
27   *him.)* Now, get on your knees. *Move!* *(He gets on his*
28   *knees.)*
29   JACK: I am, I am. You're nuts, you know that?
30   STACY: Shut up and get on your knees. Now, close your
31   eyes.
32   JACK: Omigod. What are you going to do?
33   STACY: How does this feel, Jack? How does it feel to be on
34   your knees, not knowing what I am going to do? Not
35   knowing what's going to happen next? How does it feel

1   to be completely without power?

2 JACK: You're trying to make some sort of point, I know.

3   Some sort of statement about how men treat women,

4   right?

5 STACY: Now you're getting it.

6 JACK: *(Looking right at her)* This is stupid.

7 STACY: *(Taken aback)* What?

8 JACK: This is stupid. You are so full of it. I have never done

9   anything to make a woman feel this way. Yeah, OK,

10   maybe I pushed you off a swing ten years ago. And, hey,

11   maybe some guy said he'd call and he never did. And,

12   yeah, granted, maybe you haven't been treated all that

13   great by guys. But no one ever did to you what you are

14   doing to me. You're just crazy. A crazy girl with a gun.

15   And it's probably not even loaded. *(He begins to stand.)*

16   This game is over. I'm leaving.

17 STACY: *(Raising the gun, pulling the trigger, the gun shot is*

18   *deafening.)* Think again.

19 JACK: *(Dropping to his knees)* Oh, my God.

20 STACY: Isn't it funny how we all eventually start to pray?

21   Now, where were we?

22 JACK: What do you want from me?

23 STACY: *(Evenly, thoughtfully)* I don't know. We've gone

24   down the road from annoyed to angry, then to

25   humiliated and powerless, and now we're to scared to

26   death. So far, this day has been pretty darn successful.

27   Wouldn't you say? Wouldn't you say?!

28 JACK: Yeah ... it's been great. So ... what now?

29 STACY: You tell me.

30 JACK: I don't know. How about it's over? The game is over,

31   you win, I get to go.

32 STACY: Then who will pay for the sins of men?

33 JACK: I'll tell you what. You let me go, and I will spread the

34   word. I'll tell all the men, all of them. You'll see. Come

35   on, Stacy, what would come from killing me?

1 STACY: Great personal satisfaction?
2 JACK: OK, I can see that. But, beyond that?
3 STACY: That would be enough for me.
4 JACK: There's gotta be more. Way more. You've gone to too
5   much trouble to end it like this.
6 STACY: Oh, yeah? What would you suggest, maggot?
7 JACK: Let me go. Just let me go. I won't tell anyone what
8   happened here. *(STACY raises an eyebrow.)* Or, I'll tell
9   everyone. Whatever you want. You name it. I'll do
10   whatever you want.
11 STACY: Whatever I want? Don't do me any favors. Whether
12   I let you go or not, you'll do whatever I want. I've got the
13   power here, big guy. OK. I know what I want. I want you
14   to apologize.
15 JACK: I'm sorry.
16 STACY: For what?
17 JACK: For whatever you want me to be sorry for. For not
18   calling you when I said I would. For lying to you. For
19   pushing you off the lousy swing in fifth grade. For
20   making you feel bad.
21 STACY: Do you mean it?
22 JACK: Yes. Yes, I mean it. I do. I really do.
23 STACY: *(Lowering the gun)* OK.
24 JACK: OK?
25 STACY: OK. Get out of here.
26 JACK: That's it. We're done?
27 STACY: Uh-huh. I'm really tired now.
28 JACK: I can go?
29 STACY: Yep.
30 JACK: *(Bewildered)* Just like that?
31 STACY: Uh-huh. You know what? This is over. You bore me.
32   I thought that this would be fun. It was for a while, but
33   now you bore me.
34 JACK: I bore you?
35 STACY: I thought that maybe you'd stand up, be a man. Do

1   something brave and let me see that you aren't a
2   weakling. But you crawled, you begged, you whined ...
3 JACK: But that's what you wanted.
4 STACY: That's what I *said* I wanted. It's not what I *wanted*.
5   God, you just don't understand women, do you? *(She*
6   *tosses him the gun.)* It's a starter pistol, you moron. See
7   you around. *(She leaves.)*
8 JACK: *(Examining the gun)* Omigod. Omigod.

What Do Women Want?

Cast: Kori, Alex, Jeff

Setting: At Jeff and Kori's house

Prop: Calendar

1 ALEX: So, Rita says that she can't go out with me because
2   she's busy tonight.
3 JEFF: Busy. The death word.
4 ALEX: I don't know. I've tried everything, but I don't seem
5   to be able to get anywhere.
6 JEFF: Why bother? It's a losing proposition.
7 ALEX: Women are shallow. They only want guys who are
8   good looking and spend a lot of money.
9 JEFF: Don't I know it? I took Sarah out last weekend. I
10   couldn't believe she ordered the lobster.
11 ALEX: Well, that's your fault. You shouldn't have taken her
12   to a restaurant that expensive.
13 JEFF: It's what she expected.
14 ALEX: They all expect it.
15 JEFF: And that Krista. If you asked her to the Prom she'd
16   probably want a helicopter to take you there instead of
17   a limo.
18 ALEX: They're all alike. *(He looks over at KORI who is shaking*
19   *her head just noticeably.)* What? You don't agree?
20 KORI: Saying all women are alike is the same as saying all
21   men are alike. I'm not like that.
22 JEFF: Yeah, but you're different. You're my sister.
23 ALEX: And my friend.
24 KORI: I'm still a woman.
25 JEFF: Face it, Kori. There aren't many like you.
26 ALEX: Really. If you weren't already going with Brent, I'd
27   ask you out myself.
28 JEFF: I'd ask you out, but people might talk. Incest, you

1   know, is frowned upon in this region.

2 KORI: You are both stupid.

3 ALEX: Hey, here we are saying nice things about you, and
4   you call us stupid.

5 KORI: That's because you are. You sit here talking about
6   women in general and saying all these negative things.
7   Not everyone is like Krista, you know. In fact, she is the
8   exception.

9 JEFF: Name someone who isn't that way.

10 KORI: What about Frances?

11 ALEX: Frances Stroller??? Jeff, she wants us to ask out
12   Frances Stroller.

13 JEFF: Kori, my silly little sister, Frances Stroller is not
14   exactly what we are looking for.

15 KORI: Why? What's wrong with her?

16 ALEX: She's just not our type.

17 KORI: What exactly is your type?

18 JEFF: Have you seen *Baywatch*?

19 KORI: Oh, yeah, that'll happen.

20 ALEX: It's what we aspire to.

21 JEFF: And Frances, sorry to say, will never frolic on the
22   beach with me ...

23 ALEX: Let's get a mental picture of her in a thong bikini ...

24 JEFF: I'm blind! I'm blind!!

25 KORI: You two deserve what you get.

26 ALEX: What? Why?

27 KORI: Because Frances is a great person. She's cute, nice,
28   funny, fun to be with. But no, you don't like her.

29 ALEX: I didn't say I didn't like her. I said I don't *like* her.

30 KORI: No one is telling you to marry her and have her bear
31   your children. You just might consider asking her out.

32 JEFF: "B" list, Kori, "B" list.

33 KORI: So? What's the big deal? So she's not going to be
34   Homecoming Queen. She's nice.

35 ALEX: If I want nice I will go out with you. I want hot.

1   JEFF: And while Frances may be many things ...
2   ALEX: A tad overweight being one of them ...
3   KORI: And sweet being another ...
4   ALEX and JEFF: She is not hot.
5   KORI: You know, that's what I love about you guys. You are
6   always putting down girls, saying that they only want to
7   go out with the rich, good looking guys, and here you
8   are doing exactly the same thing. It's stupid.
9   ALEX: So, what are you saying, Kori?
10   KORI: How can I make this any clearer? There are plenty of
11   attractive nice women out there who would love to do
12   something other than sit at home on a Saturday night
13   watching MTV. But no, you don't think they are hot.
14   JEFF: Kori, my pet, you are missing the point entirely.
15   KORI: I think I have hit the point on the head. You just
16   think you are too good for anyone who isn't gorgeous,
17   built like a brick house and just this side of easy.
18   JEFF: I see you do get the point.
19   KORI: Well, fine, you just keep up with that attitude. We'll
20   see how far you get with it. You know, there are a lot of
21   really nice girls who would love to go out with you.
22   JEFF: Can you blame them?
23   KORI: At this moment in time, I can say I don't understand
24   why. You are being so stupid.
25   JEFF: Stupid? Because I don't want to go out with Fat
26   Frances?
27   ALEX: We seem to be doing OK.
28   KORI: Do you Alex? Do you really?
29   ALEX: I think so.
30   KORI: So, when is the last time you had a date?
31   ALEX: Just last week.
32   KORI: With Rita, right?
33   ALEX: Yes, Rita. Why?
34   KORI: And how was it.
35   ALEX: I ... uh ... I'd prefer not to kiss and tell.

1 KORI: There's nothing to tell because there was no kissing.
2 ALEX: And how do you know?
3 KORI: Because I was with Rita the next day and she told
4   me. She said that you were nice, but not her type.
5 ALEX: I'm not good enough for her, huh?
6 JEFF: See, Kori. See, it's just like we said.
7 KORI: No, that's not what I meant. She said that you were
8   very nice, but she wants someone who wants a mature
9   relationship.
10 ALEX: Oh, so I'm immature now, huh?
11 KORI: Think about it, Alex. What did you do on your date?
12 ALEX: I took her to Nick's party.
13 KORI: And what did you do there?
14 ALEX: I saw Jeff and got a few beers ...
15 KORI: Uh-huh ... ?
16 JEFF: Didn't we play pool that night?
17 ALEX: Yeah. I won twenty-five dollars. Great night.
18 KORI: And where was Rita during this party?
19 ALEX: With me.
20 KORI: Alex, she told me what happened. You guys got to the
21   party, you went in to play pool with Jeff, and she sat
22   and watched. Then she had to drive you two home
23   because you had too much to drink.
24 JEFF: Oh, yeah, she did drive me home.
25 ALEX: Oh yeah.
26 KORI: This is not the mark of a mature man.
27 JEFF: We were having a little fun. So what?
28 ALEX: I mean, if she's going to get all freaked out by a little
29   harmless fun ...
30 KORI: Alex, idiot. You took this girl out. You were
31   responsible for her well-being. And what did you do?
32   What you would do any weekend. Hung with your
33   friends, acted like a jerk and then collapsed in a car
34   driven by someone who wasn't drinking.
35 ALEX: Hey! I had a designated driver. That's pretty

1   responsible I think.

2 JEFF: Exactly. I mean, Rita should be impressed that he

3   handled the situation so well. I know I was.

4 ALEX: Thanks, man.

5 JEFF: She should have been proud to be with you.

6 ALEX: I thought so.

7 KORI: Do me a favor.

8 ALEX: What?

9 KORI: Don't call Frances for a date. Either of you.

10 JEFF: Why?

11 KORI: She's too good for you.

12 JEFF: Oh, hey, thanks a lot.

13 KORI: I'm serious. You two sit here talking about girls and

14   how bad they treat you. I don't blame them.

15 JEFF: Thanks a lot.

16 ALEX: Great sister you have there, Jeff.

17 KORI: I'm serious. I sat here listening to you two whine and

18   moan about how mistreated you are. I almost felt sorry

19   for you. But now that I think about it, no, I don't.

20 JEFF: What did we do that was so horrible?

21 KORI: Nothing. That's just it. You don't do anything. You

22   both sit around here whining like little brats and

23   you're worse than the girls you talk about.

24 ALEX: Thanks a lot.

25 KORI: You both need to do some serious growing up. You

26   know, at first when I was talking to Rita, I tried to

27   defend you, to explain that you were just in a party

28   mood. That that was why you ignored her at Nick's

29   party.

30 ALEX: What did she say?

31 KORI: Just that she's tired of the guys at this school who

32   take the women for granted. And you know what? She's

33   right. If you want to get respect, you have to give it.

34 ALEX: Lighten up, Kori.

35 JEFF: Really. Since when are you so perfect, so mature?

1   KORI: Since listening to you two morons. The dog is more
2   mature than you. *(She exits.)*
3   ALEX: What's her problem?
4   JEFF: Check the calendar.
5   KORI: *(Re-entering)* And that's another thing. Stop making
6   stupid generalizations about women when they are
7   annoyed with you. Just because a woman is mad
8   doesn't mean that she's PMS'd out. Maybe you deserve
9   to be annoyed with. *(She exits.)*
10 JEFF: Women. They're all alike.
11   *(JEFF and ALEX start to laugh that "Women are stupid"*
12   *laugh as the scene ends.)*

Photo by Kris Alana.

Mary Krell-Oishi
and her husband Harris

About the Author

Mary Krell-Oishi has just begun her third decade teaching Theater at Sunny Hills High School in Fullerton, California. (She began teaching at the age of nine years old ... honest!) She continues to be inspired and enriched by the students who have passed through her classroom and crossed the stage.

Mary takes an enormous amount of pride and joy from the many letters and e-mails she has received from young actors from as far away as Ireland and New Zealand who have performed her short plays and have wanted to share their excitement with her. She plans to continue to write for young adults for both the stage and in fiction.

Married since 1977 to her wonderful husband, Harris, she splits her living time between Yorba Linda and Big Bear, California. As her son, Rick, is soon to be married to the lovely Shay, Mary cannot wait to have grandchildren to take to the theater, shower with gifts, spoil and send back to the unsuspecting parents.

Order Form

Meriwether Publishing Ltd.
PO Box 7710
Colorado Springs CO 80933-7710
Phone: 800-937-5297 Fax: 719-594-9916
Website: www.meriwether.com

Please send me the following books:

_____ **Scenes Keep Happening #BK-B280**   **$15.95**
by Mary Krell-Oishi
More real-life snapshots of teen lives

_____ **Scenes That Happen #BK-B156**   **$15.95**
by Mary Krell-Oishi
Dramatized snapshots of high school life

_____ **More Scenes That Happen #BK-B112**   **$14.95**
by Mary Krell-Oishi
More real-life snapshots of teenage lives

_____ **Perspectives #BK-B206**   **$14.95**
by Mary Krell-Oishi
Relevant scenes for teens

_____ **Winning Monologs for Young Actors #BK-B127** **$15.95**
by Peg Kehret
Honest-to-life monologs for young actors

_____ **Encore! More Winning Monologs for**   **$15.95**
Young Actors #BK-B144
by Peg Kehret
More honest-to-life monologs for young actors

_____ **Theatre Games for Young Performers**   **$16.95**
#BK-B188
by Maria C. Novelly
Improvisations and exercises for developing acting skills

**These and other fine Meriwether Publishing books are available at
your local bookstore or direct from the publisher. Prices subject to
change without notice. Check our website or call for current prices.**

Name: _____ e-mail: _____

Organization name: _____

Address: _____

City: _____ State: _____

Zip: _____ Phone: _____

❑ **Check enclosed**

❑ **Visa / MasterCard / Discover #** _____

Signature: _____   Expiration
                                                date: _____
                (required for credit card orders)

Colorado residents: Please add 3% sales tax.
Shipping: Include $3.95 for the first book and 75¢ for each additional book ordered.

❑ *Please send me a copy of your complete catalog of books and plays.*